adventures in
POMPOM
LanD

W9-BOB-099

Adventures in POMPOM LAND

*25 Cute Projects
Made from
Handmade Pompoms*

Myko Diann Bocek

LARK CRAFTS
Asheville

LARK CRAFTS

An Imprint of Sterling Publishing
387 Park Avenue South
New York, NY 10016

If you have questions or comments about
this book, please visit: larkcrafts.com

Editor: **Beth Sweet**
Art Director: **Kristi Pfeffer**
Layout: **Michelle Owen**
Photographer: **Jen Altman**
Cover Designer: **Kristi Pfeffer**

Library of Congress Cataloging-in-Publication Data

Bocek, Myko Diann.
  Adventures in pompom land : 25 cute projects made from handmade pompoms /
Myko Diann Bocek. -- First edition.
     pages cm
 Includes bibliographical references and index.
  ISBN 978-1-4547-0386-0
 1. Soft toys. 2. Soft toy making. I. Title.
 TT174.3.B63 2013
 745.592'4--dc23
                                    2012021395
10 9 8 7 6 5 4 3 2 1

First Edition

Published by Lark Crafts
An Imprint of Sterling Publishing Co., Inc.
387 Park Avenue South, New York, NY 10016

Text © 2013, Myko Diann Bocek
Photography © 2013, Lark Crafts, an Imprint of Sterling Publishing Co., Inc.
Illustrations © 2013, Lark Crafts, an Imprint of Sterling Publishing Co., Inc.

Distributed in Canada by Sterling Publishing,
c/o Canadian Manda Group, 165 Dufferin Street
Toronto, Ontario, Canada M6K 3H6

Distributed in the United Kingdom by GMC Distribution Services,
Castle Place, 166 High Street, Lewes, East Sussex, England BN7 1XU

Distributed in Australia by Capricorn Link (Australia) Pty Ltd.,
P.O. Box 704, Windsor, NSW 2756 Australia

The written instructions, photographs, designs, patterns, and projects in this volume
are intended for the personal use of the reader and may be reproduced for that
purpose only. Any other use, especially commercial use, is forbidden under law
without written permission of the copyright holder.

Every effort has been made to ensure that all the information in this book is
accurate. However, due to differing conditions, tools, and individual skills, the
publisher cannot be responsible for any injuries, losses, and other damages that may
result from the use of the information in this book.

Some of the terms included in the book may be trademarks or registered
trademarks. Use of such terms does not imply any association with or endorsement
by such trademark owners and no association or endorsement is intended or should
be inferred. This book is not authorized by, and neither the Author nor the Publisher
is affiliated with the owners of the trademarks referred to in the book.

Manufactured in China

All rights reserved

ISBN 13: 978-1-4547-0386-0

For information about custom editions, special sales, and premium and corporate
purchases, please contact Sterling Special Sales Department at 800-805-5489 or
specialsales@sterlingpub.com.

Requests for information about desk and examination copies available to college and
university professors must be submitted to academic@larkbooks.com. Our complete
policy can be found at www.larkcrafts.com.

Dedication

This book is in loving memory of my late father,
who always encouraged me to pursue my love of art.

Contents

THE PROJECTS

Introduction

Back in 2000 I fell in love with an article in *Martha Stewart Living* magazine about making pompom animals from handmade pompoms. My children were much younger at the time; we created a few, had immense fun, and took great pleasure in making them. Then in 2007 I was watching Martha Stewart's television show and was inspired once more after a segment that featured Jennifer Murphy making little pompom bunnies. Again, I made some. Over the next couple years my work evolved, and I began to create my own pompom animal designs. As I started creating again, I was filled with joy in rediscovering my artistic passion! Friends and family loved my little woolen creatures, and they encouraged me to continue in my pursuits, which I gratefully did. That creative path has led me to my own online shop and the authorship of this book.

In *Adventures in Pompom Land*, you'll learn all about making pompoms by hand, and you'll find yourself in the company of creatures of all kinds: from a mischievous masked Raccoon and a softly-spiked Hedgehog to a gentle-eyed Lamb and an elegant Swan. Say hello to springtime with a sweet Yellow Chick, have years of good luck with a Halloween Black Cat, and celebrate winter with the charming Snowman and Snowgirl duo. Pompom creatures make perfect heartfelt gifts for loved ones and friends as holiday presents and ornaments, wedding cake toppers, home décor, heirloom treasures, pincushions—the list goes on and on.

The 25 projects in this book all reference basic techniques explained in the Pompom-Making Essentials, which walks you step-by-step through the process of winding, tying, cutting, fluffing, and shaping a pompom by hand. You'll learn how to make multi-colored pompoms, how to shape a pompom into smaller head shapes and larger body shapes, how to add armatures, and how to create a cute expression for your creature with the easy placement of facial details. You'll also learn the basics of needle felting, which is a technique used to form some of the projects' tails, legs, and feet.

Once you get the hang of making a pompom, you'll realize how versatile this craft can be—let these projects inspire your imagination and discover how your creativity unfolds into personalized, beloved pompom creatures for all occasions.

Myko Diann Bocek

Pompom-Making Essentials

Welcome to Pompom Land! The sweet and expressive projects in this book are all created with a few basic supplies and a few easy-to-learn techniques. Once you get into the groove of making pompoms, the sky's the limit when it comes to dreaming up cute critters and scenes for your very own Pompom Land.

Pompom Materials and Tools

There are a few materials you'll need on hand to form the elements of your pompom creatures, and they can all be sourced from craft supply stores. In fact, many of them are probably already among your crafting supplies at home!

100% Wool Yarn and 100% Wool Roving Yarn

All of the projects in this book use 100% wool yarn, wool felt, and wool roving. I can find basic wool yarn colors at my craft store, but if you want to use other custom shades be sure to visit a local yarn shop because they usually have a larger selection. I have also tried my hand at dyeing my own wool with powdered clothing dye you can mix in a tub or your washing machine. (Wool roving and felt can also be dyed to match, if necessary. Simply follow the directions on the package to make custom colors.) If you choose to dye your yarn, synthetic or synthetic-blend yarn will not take dye well, if at all. Using 100% wool gives your handcrafted animals that rich heirloom-like vintage quality.

Several projects call for the use of wool roving yarn. This yarn is not twisted like traditional yarn. It is much fluffier and chunkier. It is wonderful for use in certain projects to add dimension, and it also adds to the illusion in creating fluffy feathers, manes, and tails.

✳ **NOTE:** *Roving yarn is different from wool roving, which is described in the Needle Felting Supplies section on page 16.*

100% Wool Felt

Wool felt can be purchased in different millimeter thicknesses. I like to use the 2 to 3 mm thickness for the ears, but regular 1 mm wool felt works just as well. Using synthetic felt will not give you the same results. Synthetic felt does not hold up well over time; it will pill and stretch out and generally does not look as nice as pure wool felt.

Cardboard Sleeve

You will need a strong, flat, smooth piece of cardboard approximately 5 x 3 inches (12.7 x 7.6 cm) to wrap the bundle of yarn around to create the pompoms. If you are feeling really industrious, I suggest you cut out a thin piece of plywood commonly used for making dollhouses, which will hold up better over time. Lightly sand the edges so the yarn will not catch on any rough spots when you slide it off the board, which can ruin your pompom. It's also helpful to wrap packing tape around the edges of the sleeve, which will help the yarn slide off easier.

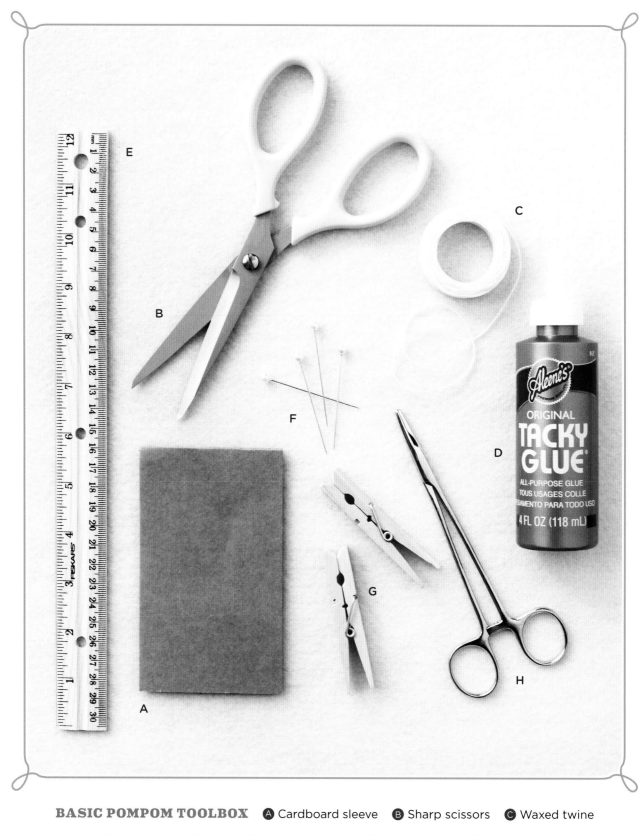

BASIC POMPOM TOOLBOX   Ⓐ Cardboard sleeve   Ⓑ Sharp scissors   Ⓒ Waxed twine

Ⓓ Adhesives   Ⓔ Ruler   Ⓕ Long floral pins   Ⓖ Clothespins or Ⓗ hemostats

Sharp Scissors

Trimming and sculpting the pompoms takes a lot of cutting, and it is necessary to have good-quality scissors. A pair of nice, strong, *sharp* scissors helps immensely in cutting and trimming pompoms. Weak, flimsy scissors will not consistently cut smoothly through the wool yarn. Also, your wrist and hand will tire quickly. Cheap, dull scissors will "chew" and pull the yarn out of your knotted pompom, which results in sloppy, uneven work. Cutting wool is essentially cutting hair, which can dull your scissors over time, so you may need to sharpen them occasionally.

Waxed Twine

To tie off the pompoms I use white waxed twine, which is found in the jewelry section of craft stores. Using the waxed twine keeps your knots from slipping loose while tightening the knot to secure the yarn bundle. It is essential to tie a knot as tightly as possible to create a good, fluffy pompom.

Adhesives

I prefer to use white craft glue for creating my little animals, and I've found tacky glue works the best. Don't be tempted to use hot glue when attaching pompoms, no matter how easy it may seem. Hot glue hardens very quickly after it's applied, and it seeps through the fibers of a pompom to create hard, stringy strands that you won't be able to cut away. It will also create a thick, hard disc of glue within your pompoms, which will permanently mat the yarn's fibers together. Also, since you'll be arranging and attaching pompoms by hand, hot glue can burn your fingers. Craft glue is your friend!

Long Floral Pins

Long floral pins help temporarily hold pompoms in place when you glue them together. These are the same pins used for wearing corsages or boutonnieres, and they can be found in the floral supply section of craft stores. When the glue holding pompoms together has dried completely, gently twist and pull the floral pin to remove it.

Clothespins or Hemostats

Clothespins are handy tools for securely holding glued felt together while the glue dries. This will be most helpful when you're pinching the bottom edge of a felt ear ❶ or creating a folded felt beak. If you'd like to try another option, hemostats are clamping instruments commonly used in the medical field. They can be found in some craft stores or sporting goods stores (fishermen often use them to remove hooks from fish), and they'll also do a good job of securely pressing felt to hold it in shape while the glue dries.

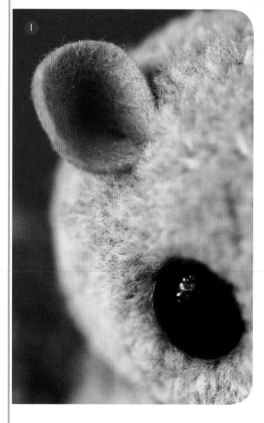

Pompom-Making Essentials

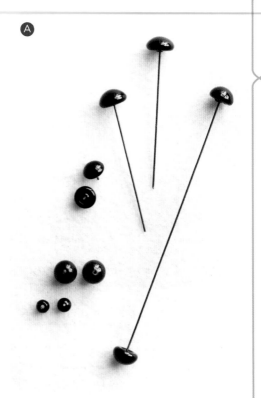

❀ NOTE: *As with any craft including small, hard elements, glass eyes may pose a choking hazard to young children.*

Glass Eyes

The projects in this book were made with glass eyes commonly used in teddy bear and doll assembly Ⓐ. These eyes come in pairs: some are securely attached to a wire stem with one eye on each end, and others are attached to wire loops. For the eyes on wire stems, simply use wire cutters to snip the wire to about ½ inch (1.3 cm) below the glass eye. Squeeze glue into the pompom where you'd like to place an eye, and insert the wire into the pompom fibers and glue.

Glass eyes come in a variety of colors, shapes, and sizes: I prefer to use the all-black glass eyes ranging between 10mm an 14mm in diameter. Not all craft stores carry glass eyes, so see the Resource section (page 125) for a few suggestions of retailers that sell them.

Don't want to use glass eyes for your pompom creatures? No problem. Instead, use black glass or onyx beads from your local craft store or bead shop.

Wire Cutters

Wire cutters are handy for a multitude of reasons when creating your projects! You can get a few different sizes for different uses. Larger ones are needed for more heavy-duty cutting (of wooden dowels, for example) and smaller ones for cutting pipe cleaners and thin floral wire.

Embroidery Floss

Embroidery floss serves several uses. To make the wrapped wire feet on the birds and chicks, I use the heavier floss (perle cotton), which has a slight sheen. You can also use the floss to hang little signs or gift tags from your animals. They come in a wide variety of beautiful colors.

Ribbons

Choosing the right ribbon also makes a big difference. It cannot be too stiff or heavy, and it should be scaled to the size of your woolen pompom animal. I prefer silk ribbon because it is very light, pliable, and beautiful. I also use 12 mm seam-binding ribbon for the perfect vintage-inspired finishing touch. I also like 4 mm velvet and delicate lace ribbons.

Floral Supplies

I like to use vintage millinery supplies that I scavenge at thrift stores and yard sales. Many can be found online as well. I find the paper forget-me-not flowers are the perfect size and scale for the pompom animals. Velvet leaves are also a staple and can be found easily online. For a dainty feminine touch, you can glue a tiny millinery forget-me-not flower and/or a leaf at your pompom animal's ear.

Floral wire and tape are also valuable in creating certain projects. I use the floral wire to create feet for the birds and arches on bases. The tape I use for wrapping the stems of millinery flowers when making a tiny bouquet.

Making Clothes for Your Pompom Creatures

You can certainly sew some adorable little clothes for your animals. I like to make simple outfits that do not require a lot of sewing. I have created little top hats and scarves out of wool felt, such as on the Snowman and Snowgirl (page 116) and little bonnets out of velvet millinery flowers and leaves, such as on the Bluebird (page 48). You can cut simple vests out of wool felt and make little skirts out of a wide piece of lace. The ideas are endless!

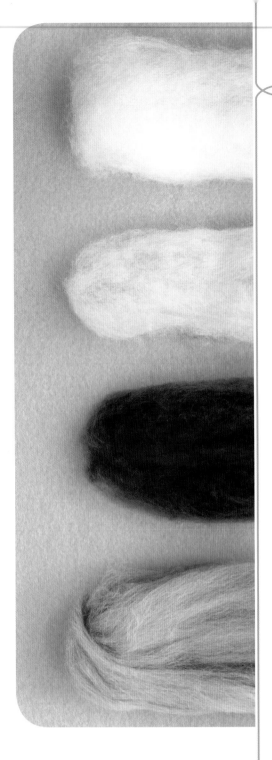

Needle Felting Supplies

Many of the pompom creatures in this book have needle-felted appendages such as little arms, legs, paws, and tails. The needle felting technique is quite simple: use a felting needle to repeatedly pierce layers of wool roving; the barbs on the felting needle catch hold of the fibers in the wool and enmesh them together to create a firm, dense shape. The supplies described below can be found at your local craft store and online. There are many varieties and brands of tools; feel free to experiment with different types of needles and work surfaces to see what suits your preference.

100% Wool Roving

Wool roving is wool that has been carded, or combed, so the fibers are all oriented in the same direction, and then it is gently twisted into a soft, springy bundle (it's not yet twisted into yarn). I use 100% wool roving in my work, and it can be found in craft stores and online in many colors. Measuring and working with roving isn't extremely precise, and the density of your needle-felted appendages depends on the amount of roving you use and how much you needle felt it. But once you begin adding roving to an armature or rolling it together, you'll realize how easy it is to simply add more layers of roving to your work until it reaches the desired density.

✳ **NOTE**: *When you use wool roving in your projects, gently pull a strip of it from the bundle; don't cut it with scissors.*

Felting Needles

Felting needles are barbed steel needles used to interlock the fibers of wool. As you move the felting needle up and down, the barbs on the needle catch the fibers of wool roving and blend them together, compressing them into felt. These needles have incredibly sharp points, so be sure to keep them away from children and use caution as you work with them. They're usually about 3 1/2 to 4 inches (8.9 to 10.2 cm) long and come in a variety of sizes and gauges. The gauge is indicated by number; the higher the number, the finer the needle.

I like using a pen-style felting needle tool, which allows you to use one, two, three, and sometimes even four needles at once to needle felt areas of varying measurements. The needle sizes and lengths can be adjusted in a pen-style tool, and I find that they're quite easy to hold and control, especially when the needles are set close together.

Work Surface for Needle Felting

You'll need a work surface specifically for needle felting that will allow your needle to go through the fiber (and beyond it) without puncturing the work surface or breaking the needle. I use a large brush felting mat to work on my projects, and I find it's especially helpful in making small ears, feet, and tails. There are also dense foam surfaces created especially for needle felting, and some people like to use upholstery foam to support their work.

Pipe Cleaners

I like to use pipe cleaners rather than floral wire for the armature frames of appendages. The chenille on the pipe cleaner grabs the roving and keeps it from spinning as you needle felt. I order 100% cotton chenille pipe cleaners online, but you can use any coordinating-color pipe cleaners easily found at the craft store. You'll want to use like colors in your projects, as dark colors can show through light-colored roving, and vice versa. If you need to tint the color of your pipe cleaner, simply rub a piece of chalk into its fibers for a quick fix.

Also, for some pompom animals (such as the Mouse, page 38, and the Halloween Imp, page 103), you do not need to needle felt the tail. You can just simply use the pipe cleaner and trim one end to a point. Be sure to trim any sharp metal wire edges of the pipe cleaner with your wire cutters.

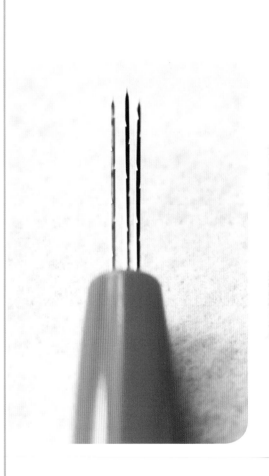

STASH IDEA

A time-saving tip is to make a stash of pompoms for future use. I like to wind and tie off pompom bundles while watching television and set them aside for later. I also get my kids and husband to pitch in once in a while! Bribery often works wonders.

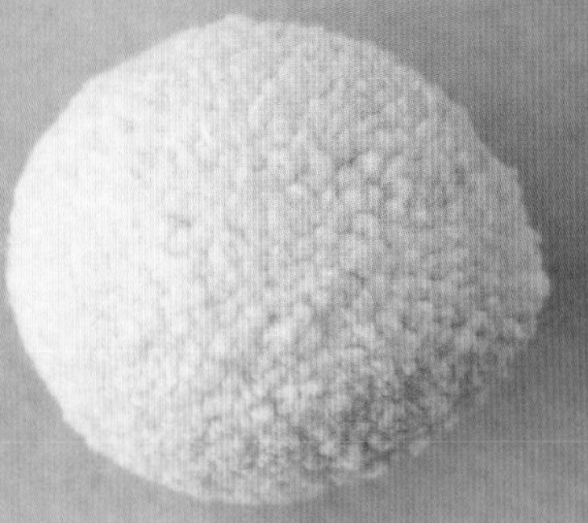

Making Pompoms by Hand

1. Choosing Your Yarn

There are many types of wool yarn on the market. I like to use a cream color yarn made by Patons for the majority of my projects. It's springy, it takes dye for custom colors nicely, it's not too thin, and it's readily available at many craft stores at reasonable prices. For other projects I use wool roving yarn. This yarn is not twisted like traditional yarn; instead, it is loosely spun. It creates a chunkier and fluffier effect. This yarn works nicely for creating feathers for birds such as the Snowy Owl (page 100) and Swan (page 71). It also comes in handy for the tails of the Squirrel (page 80) and Hedgehog (page 88). Experiment with different yarns to find just the look you want for your animal.

I have made all of the projects in this book with either Patons Classic Wool yarn or Patons Classic Wool Roving yarn, though the approximate yarn measurements I reference in the project instructions are meant to apply to any brand of yarn or roving yarn. The wool yarn I've used is medium weight and comes in 3 1/2-ounce (100 g) skeins measuring 210 yards (192 m). The wool roving yarn I've used is bulky weight and comes in 3 1/2-ounce (100 g) skeins measuring 120 yards (109 m).

In my project instructions, I've provided the yardage needed and referenced fractions of skeins based on the amount and type of yarn I've used. You should feel free to experiment with different brands and types of yarn, so here's an approximate comparison you can apply to any brand of yarn:

100% Wool Yarn

1 skein of Patons 100% wool yarn, *Classic Wool*		210 yards (192 m)
1/8 skein of Patons 100% wool yarn	IS EQUIVALENT TO	26 yards (24 m)
1/4 skein of Patons 100% wool yarn		53 yards (48 m)
1/3 skein of Patons 100% wool yarn		69 yards (63 m)
1/2 skein of Patons 100% wool yarn		105 yards (96 m)
2/3 skein of Patons 100% wool yarn		139 yards (127 m)
3/4 skein of Patons 100% wool yarn		158 yards (144 m)

100% Wool Roving Yarn

1 skein of Patons 100% wool roving yarn, *Classic Wool Roving*		120 yards (109 m)
¼ skein of Patons 100% wool roving yarn		30 yards (27 m)
⅓ skein of Patons 100% wool roving yarn	IS EQUIVALENT TO	40 yards (36 m)
½ skein of Patons 100% wool roving yarn		60 yards (55 m)
⅔ skein of Patons 100% wool roving yarn		79 yards (72 m)
¾ skein of Patons 100% wool roving yarn		90 yards (82 m)

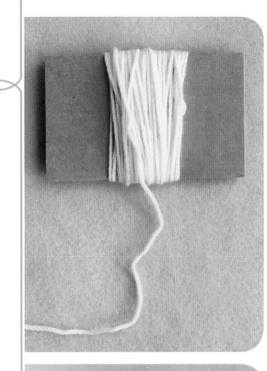

2. Wrap Yarn around the Cardboard Sleeve

Beginning in the center of the cardboard sleeve, wrap the yarn around and around with consistent and gentle tension. Gradually alternate the yarn from left to right, keeping it centered and evenly distributed. Try not to wrap the yarn too tightly, because it will be difficult to slide it off of the cardboard sleeve in the next step.

For pompoms made of more than one color, wrap the first color uniformly as you would a regular pompom, and then wrap the second color directly next to—but not overlapping—the first color. (See Making Multicolor Pompoms, page 30, for some tips.)

It's okay if you run out of yarn while you're wrapping: simply continue wrapping (in the same direction) with a new strand of yarn until you've reached the thickness and density you need for your pompom.

3. Slide Yarn off the Cardboard Sleeve

After you've wrapped the yarn around the cardboard sleeve, gently slide the bundle off one end of the sleeve. The yarn should retain its dense bundled shape; keep it intact.

4. Tie the Yarn Bundle with Waxed Twine

I use waxed twine to tie off my yarn bundles when making pompoms. The wax on the twine prevents the knot from slipping loose; you need to tie it as tightly as possible to make your

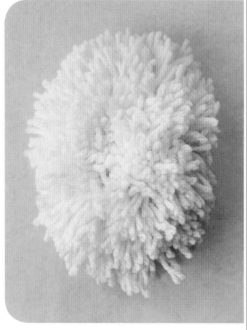

pompom fluffy and to prevent the yarn from pulling loose after you snip the looped ends. Before wrapping the yarn around the cardboard sleeve, I usually cut the twine in 12- to 14-inch (30.5 to 35.6 cm) lengths so that when I slide the bundle off, I can lay the bundle down on it. Then tie a simple knot and tighten it as much as possible. Next, flip the bundle over to its other side and, using the excess twine from the first knot, tie another knot. Again tighten it as much as possible. Then make a double knot to secure it. Trim the twine.

5. Cut the Pompom's Loops

Once you've tied your wrapped bundle of yarn tightly, slide the blade of your scissors into the loops at one end of the bundle. Gently tug the loops taut so they're all roughly the same length, and then snip through them. Repeat this step on the loops of the bundle's other end. Now, instead of a tied bundle of loops, you'll have the fluffy beginnings of a pompom.

6. Shape the Pompom

The main point to keep in mind when shaping a pompom is to work *gradually*. It's kind of like trimming a bonsai tree or pruning shrubs—make small cuts as you go. To sculpt and shape a pompom into a smooth ball, one of my techniques is to constantly flip and turn the ball while cutting. I also constantly rake the yarn ends with the blade of my scissors as I trim to fluff up any stray strands of yarn that need to be trimmed down. As you trim and cut, picture the shape in your mind that you want to create.

The most common shape I use for the pompom animal's head is a small egg shape. It lends itself well to practically almost every animal design. As you become more experienced you can make slight variations to create other head or body shapes for different animals.

I often shape the body into a pear shape, meaning the bottom half is thicker and heavier (like the bottom of a pear) and the top tapers off to a more narrow shape, half of which will be the neck and shoulders of your animal. The larger pompoms already resemble a large hourglass shape after cutting the looped ends, so by simply trimming away the excess yarn you can begin to see the body shape in rough form. Just continue trimming down, pausing to stop and look periodically as you sculpt.

For many of the animals, you can create the illusion of its haunches, knees, and tummy as it sits by cutting a V shape from the front center bottom of the belly area. At the base of the pompom, the V shape should measure approximately 1 inch (2.5 cm) wide, 1½ inches (3.8 cm) long, and ¼ inch (6 mm) deep; these measurements are very rough and will depend on the size of the pompoms you make and sculpt. There really is no right or wrong here. Sculpt and trim the yarn to shape the front of the body pompom; the sides of the V can curve a bit to form the belly and haunches.

TIPS ON SHAPING THE NOSE AND MUZZLE

For many of the creatures, after making and roughly forming the head pompom into the appropriate size and shape (usually an egg shape), you can trim and cut out a pointed nose in the lower center half of the head pompom.

Determine the top and the bottom of the head, and position the nose a bit lower than the center of the pompom. Begin to trim and shape the pointed area where the nose will be. Depending on the animal, the nose may be very pointy, like the Fox (page 92), or a little more rounded, like the Mouse (page 38).

For some animals, such as the Puppy (page 67), Piglet (page 77), and Teddy Bear (page 60), trim the yarn a bit deeper on the top half of the head just above the snout or muzzle area, as shown below. This creates a more realistic shape for the nose.

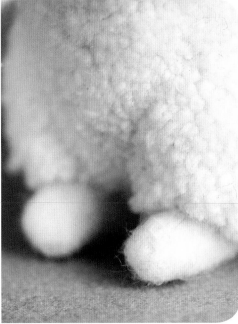

Adding Facial Features

Positioning the Nose and Eyes

After you have trimmed the head into the desired shape, use an upside-down triangle pattern to determine where you want the nose and eyes to be (the nose will be at the bottom of the inverted triangle). Squeeze a small drop of glue into the pompom fibers for the nose and gently insert the nose bead. If you're using glass eyes on a wire stem, use wire cutters to trim the wire to about ½ inch (1.3 cm) below the glass eye. If you're using glass eyes with a wire loop in the back, keep the loop in its original shape. Carefully squeeze a pea-size drop of glue for each eye into the fibers of the pompom and gently nestle the wire end of the eye into the pompom. If you're using glass beads for your creature's eyes, position them so the holes of the beads are not exposed or visible. Let the glue dry completely.

Creating and Attaching Whiskers

Purchase upholstery thread at a craft or fabric store. It is thicker and stronger than regular thread. Sometimes, the thread curls when you take it off the spool, so I like to thread my needle with a double strand and then take my flat iron (or household iron) to straighten the thread before use. Make a knot in the center of the double strand and place a smidge of glue on the knot. I usually insert the threaded needle through the cheeks and just under the nose; the glued knot will catch somewhere near the middle of the head. Then I simply cut the threads evenly to the desired length on each side of the head.

Creating and Attaching Wool Felt Ears

Wool felt comes in different thicknesses. The thinner wool felt is easier to use and manipulate, though I prefer thicker felt for my pompom creatures. I'll often pinch and glue the bottom edges of felt ears together before inserting them into the pompom, which gives the ears expressive dimension. When using the thicker wool, clothespins or hemostats are needed to hold the pinched, glued edges together until dry. After determining the exact location where I want the ears to be, I use the sharp, pointy end of my scissors to make a deep part into the wool "fur." I then squeeze the glue into the part before permanently securing the ears by pinching the wool fibers around them.

❋ **NOTE:** *Use pink chalk to add a little color to some projects' ears.*

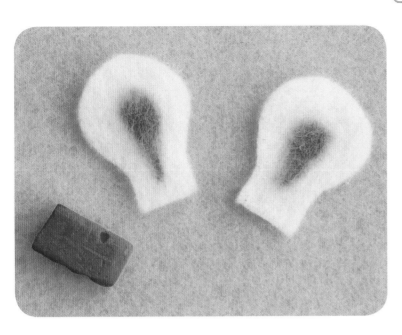

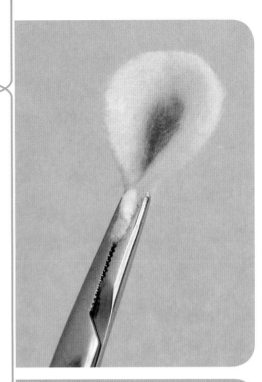

Using Templates

In the back of the book, you'll find the templates you need to make ears and other small shapes for the pompom creatures. Copy the templates onto paper and cut them out. Place the paper shape(s) onto the felt and either trace them with an air-soluble fabric-marking pen (the ink disappears after exposure to air for a length of time), or hold or pin them in place and cut around them. Try to cut the shapes in one fluid motion, which will prevent ragged or uneven edges in the details.

Attaching Pompoms

Attaching pompoms to one another is quite simple, especially since you need only a few tools: pompoms, glue, a long floral pin, and patience. You'll essentially be gluing the pompoms together and giving the glue plenty of time to set up.

To attach a pompom head to a pompom body, make a part in the yarn at the top of the body pompom and squeeze a nickel-size dollop of glue into the part. (If your critter features arms made from pipe-cleaner armatures, attach the pipe cleaners *before* gluing on the head. You can needle felt the wool roving on the arms after you've attached the head.) Align and position the head pompom to your liking, and press it onto the glue. To keep the head and body from detaching before the glue sets up, use a long floral pin to hold them in place. Remove the pin after the glue has set up.

Pompom-Making Essentials

❋ **NOTE:** *You'll add the appendage armature(s) **before** attaching the head and body pompoms together, but you'll needle felt the armature(s) **after** you've attached the head and body together.*

Creating Appendages

Most of the creatures in this book have appendages made by needle felting wool roving to pipe cleaner armatures like the Mouse's arms (page 38). Other creatures have appendages made by needle felting wool roving to thin wooden dowels like the Lamb's legs (page 63). Some of the smaller appendages, like the Puppy's back paws (page 67), are made without armatures of any kind.

Adding an Armature

This step is actually easier than you may think. All you need are a pipe cleaner and glue! I simply make a deep part in the top of the neck and shoulder area, squeeze some glue into the part, and then wedge the pipe cleaner down into the glue. I then pinch the wool fibers around the pipe cleaner to secure and let it dry. Just remember to glue the pipe cleaner armatures in *first* before the head or you will have to start over! Also, it is natural to want to finish your creature *before* letting the glue dry. Be patient. Let the glue dry, because disturbing it before it sets up will ruin the pompom.

Wrapping an Armature in Roving

❋ **NOTE:** *When your pompom critter is made of multiple pompoms, attach the head and body pompoms to one another (and let the glue dry fully!) **before** you needle felt the pipe cleaner armatures for appendages.*

To needle felt over a pipe cleaner armature after the glue has set up, pull off a piece of roving the size of a thick strip of bacon and wrap it tightly around the pipe cleaner arms Ⓐ Ⓑ. Use more roving near the upper arm and shoulder area and taper it off at the end to form a paw. As you needle felt the roving with your needle tool, the fibers will compress, and you will wrap and needle felt more layers of roving around your armature until it is the right size.

Needle Felting Appendages

The needle felting technique is quite simple and favors repetition. Simply insert your felting needle straight down into the layers of wool roving and then extract it through the same hole, working straight up and down Ⓒ. As the needle moves in and out of the roving, the barbs grasp and push the fibers in the wool and enmesh them together to create a firm, dense, compact shape.

When you're creating appendages for the pompom creatures, make sure you needle felt the roving tightly and compactly around any armature so the roving will not unravel. Flip the pompom creature over and around on the felting mat so you can access every angle of the appendage Ⓓ. (This is why you need to wait until any glue on the creature is completely dry—all that flipping

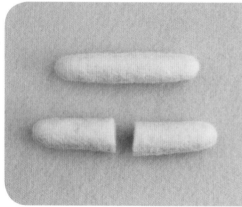

and rotating might detach an unsecured head or other detail!) Simply keep adding layers of wool roving to the appendage until you have formed your desired shape and size. Tuck any stray, loose ends of roving into the fibers of the pompom and gently needle felt them in place.

Creating Needle-Felted Tails

To make a thick, long tail, take a pipe cleaner and wrap roving around it, with more roving at the base where it will attach to the body and becoming thinner at the tail's tip. Place it on the needle felting mat and begin needle felting. Needle felt it until it is nice and compact; trim off any excess or stray roving fibers with a pair of sharp scissors. To make a smaller, more rounded tail like the Bunny's (page 35), roll a piece of roving into a marble-size ball and needle felt it, adding layers of roving as necessary.

Attaching Feet and Small Appendages

Inserting the bottom feet is easy enough. Needle felt a piece of roving into a tight, compact cigar shape and cut it in half. Make two parts into the bottom of the pompom where you want the feet to go, each about ½ inch (1.3 cm) deep. Place a line of glue in each and then gently push in the feet, leaving the rounded toe end sticking out at the front of the body. Set the animal upright to get the right angle so that it stands, and let the glue dry. Be sure not to place the animal directly on a table that can be ruined by glue adhering to it while the animal is drying.

❋ **NOTE:** *Use this simple gluing technique to adhere other small appendages to pompoms, such as the Bunny's tail.*

Making Bases

You can create a variety of unique and wonderful little bases for your animals with relative ease. Small bases can showcase a special pompom creation and can be quite charming. A larger base can house two or more animals, and you can create little vignettes or perhaps even a wedding cake topper. For some pompom creations, like the Squirrel (page 80), the base provides stability for an otherwise asymmetrical creature.

You can find small, unfinished wooden disks at your local craft store in different diameters and thicknesses. I like to use pieces 3 to 4 inches (7.6 to 10.2 cm) in diameter. Paint them in any color you desire. You can also decoupage them with vintage paper found in old books, or coat them with glue and add glass glitter (see the Halloween Black Cat, page 109). To add more dimension and soften the wooden disk's look, rather than leaving the painted wood bare, I prefer to cut out, with scalloped-edge or zigzag pinking scissors, a round piece of 3 mm wool felt that is slightly larger than the wooden disk and glue it to the wood (see the Snowman and Snowgirl, page 116).

Polystyrene foam floral disks are also a staple of mine when creating bases. They, too, are found in a wide variety of sizes and shapes. Let your imagination run wild! You can cover the flat foam disk with wool felt. Use vintage trim, rickrack, or ribbon to embellish the edge. After attaching your animal to the base, you can add millinery flowers and leaves.

I have also found cute papier-mâché boxes at my local craft store to paint and embellish. Topped with a little woolen pompom creature, these make special gifts as well as keepsake boxes. Again, paint these and add bits of ribbon, lace, trim, glitter, and/or millinery flowers.

When I am out hunting in my local thrift and antique shops I like to look for old-fashioned bun-shaped pincushions. These make great vintage-inspired bases for your pompom animals, and they're a wonderful gift for that friend who likes to sew. Simply glue your animal to the top, and you have a sweet and useful pincushion. Glue a little spool of thread in your animal's paws for an added touch of cuteness!

If you are comfortable with needle felting (see page 24), needle felt a base for your critter, like I did for the Mouse paddling in a Leaf Boat on page 38. I have created wonderful red-and-white polka-dotted mushrooms for my little mice to sit upon, or a mossy little cushion for a bunny to enjoy. Again, the sky's the limit!

Tips and Troubleshooting Guide

Using Enough Yarn

One of the easiest mistakes to make while creating pompoms is not using enough yarn. It is very important that the pompoms be *extremely* dense and full in order to sculpt them and so they're able to support some of the added features such as the Elephant's trunk and the Fox's tail. Most of the animals in this book are between 5 and 6½ inches (12.7 and 16.5 cm) tall, and it will take about one-third of the yarn skein to make the head and almost half of the skein to create the body of most of the creatures included in these pages. If there is not enough yarn used, the pompom will be limp and skimpy, and will not give you the desired results.

Tying Knots

It can be a bit tricky to tie the knot as tightly as possible for your pompoms. As described on page 13, using waxed twine will help you immensely. There have been times when I was tying a knot as tightly as I could, and the twine broke. You can still salvage the pompom: keep the pompom intact and simply retie it again with another piece of waxed twine. It might be a good idea to cut a couple of 12- to 14-inch (30.5 to 35.6 cm) lengths of waxed twine before you start winding the pompom. The twine can cut your fingers similar to paper, so use care when tightly pulling and tying.

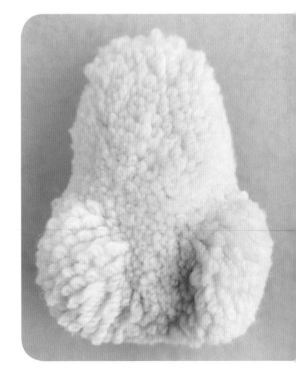

Shaping Pompoms

To sculpt and shape a pompom into a smooth ball, one of my techniques is to constantly flip and turn the ball while cutting. I also constantly "rake" the yarn ends with the blade of my scissors as I trim to fluff up any stray strands of yarn that need to be trimmed down. This is a very gradual process, and the most reliable way to achieve a symmetrical, controlled shape is to trim the pompom with small snips. Think of this like a haircut—once you've cut something, you can't get it back!

To create the illusion of the animal's haunches, you will trim a V shape of yarn from the front bottom center of the body's (usually)

pear shape to create the illusion of a tummy and to sculpt the haunches and knees of the sitting animal on each side. The width at the very base of the V is approximately 1 inch (2.5 cm), which is trimmed about $1/4$ inch (6 mm) lower than the surrounding yarn or "fur." The height of the V shape is about $1 1/2$ inches (3.8 cm), and the sides can curve a bit to form the rounded belly area. Start smaller and trim more yarn, if desired, as you sculpt this body pompom. It might take a little practice to perfect this technique, but hang in there—you'll soon be shaping pompom haunches like a pro!

Making Multicolor Pompoms

One of the most complex techniques to master is combining multiple yarn colors in a pompom, but once you can see how the wrapped multicolor yarn bundle slides off the cardboard sleeve and translates into a tied pompom, you'll be able to manipulate and shape a multicolor pompom with ease.

With most multicolor pompoms, you should wrap the different colors side by side, not overlapping each other. After you become a bit experienced making pompoms, you will notice how the yarn in the pompom bundle unfolds and opens when the looped ends are cut. Shape the pompom so that the colors stay separate

within the pompom: a great example is the Hedgehog (page 88), which has dark brown and cream yarn in its head. I kept the dark brown yarn a bit longer than the cream yarn as I trimmed the pompom: the result is a "smooth" cream face, while the back of its dark brown head looks "spiky." Another good example is the Fox (page 92), which has an orange and cream head. For projects like these, you can gently tweak and tug the different colors of yarn into place before you begin shaping the pompom. This might take some practice, but don't feel discouraged if your first attempts aren't exactly what you have in mind. Part of the beauty of making pompoms by hand is the satisfaction you'll feel when you transform plain old yarn into a dense, dimensional shape. Be patient with your efforts and have fun—you're creating some seriously cute creatures!

Yellow Chick

Little chicks are so adorable: they're perfect to make for spring and celebrating new life. Make a few to adorn your home, tuck in an Easter basket, or give as special gifts this year. Use these same directions to also create ducklings by rounding the beak and wrapping the embroidery floss or perle cotton around the wire feet to create a webbed appearance.

1. Following steps 2–6 of Making Pompoms by Hand on pages 19–21, make a 2½-inch (6.4 cm) round ball-shaped pompom from yellow yarn for the head. I used approximately ¼ skein of Patons medium-weight Classic Wool, which is approximately 53 yards (48 m).

2. Using the template on page 121, cut out a beak from orange wool felt.

3. Locate where you want the beak to be on the ball-shaped pompom. Make a small part into the pile of the yarn and place a small drop of glue there. Insert the wool felt beak. Pinch the fibers around the glue and wool felt beak to secure it.

4. Using the inverted triangle layout (see Positioning the Nose and Eyes on page 22), decide where you want the eyes to be. Make a part in the yarn, carefully squeeze in a pea-size drop of glue for each eye, and gently insert the wire end of each glass eye into the pompom. Let the glue dry.

YOU WILL NEED

Basic Pompom Toolbox
(page 12)

100% wool yarn:
yellow

100% wool felt:
orange

Template: beak
(page 121)

2 black glass eyes,
10 or 12 mm

Wire cutters

32 inches (81.3 cm) of
18-gauge floral wire

Embroidery floss or perle
cotton: yellow or orange

Ribbon

Millinery flowers

FINISHED MEASUREMENTS
4 ¾ inches (12 cm) tall

Yellow Chick

5. Make another slightly larger pompom from yellow yarn and trim it into an egg shape for the body, about 3½ inches (8.9 cm) long. I used approximately ⅓ skein of Patons medium-weight Classic Wool, which is approximately 69 yards (63 m). Sculpt and trim the tail end into a soft point.

6. Glue the finished head onto the body. To create a cute, inquisitive expression, tilt the head to one side. Squeeze a nickel-size dollop of glue at the top of the body pompom and position the head as desired. You will need to let the glue set up and dry, which can take a few hours. To keep the head from falling off before the glue sets up, use a long floral pin to hold it in place. Remove the pin after the glue has set up.

7. Using wire cutters, cut eight 4-inch (10.2 cm) pieces of floral wire.

8. To create the legs, take four pieces of wire, hold them together, and lightly coat the bundle with glue. Working from top to bottom, wind the embroidery floss or perle cotton tightly and uniformly around the wires. Stop approximately 1½ inches (3.8 cm) from the bottom. Bend each of the four wires out at a 90° angle to make individual toes. Three will face forward; one will face backward to provide the support needed for the chick to stand. Continue wrapping each "toe" wire individually with embroidery floss to cover the floral wire. Repeat with the remaining four pieces of floral wire to create the other leg. Use wire cutters to snip off any excess wire length. Tuck any ends of embroidery floss underneath and let the glue dry.

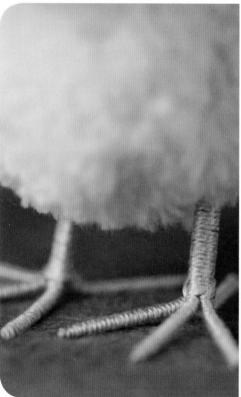

9. At the bottom of the Chick's body, make two separate parts into the wool plush for the legs and squeeze a dollop of glue into each. Insert the wire legs into the body. Pinch the wool fibers around the wrapped wires to secure them. Set the Chick upright and make any adjustments necessary so that it can dry standing upright.

10. Embellish your Chick with a ribbon and millinery flowers.

❋ **NOTE:** *The top hat described on page 115 can also be used for your little Chick.*

Bunny

Baby bunnies are adorable and hard to resist. They're also my favorite animals to make and a favorite for gift giving during spring and Easter time.

Basic Pompom Toolbox
(page 12)

100% wool yarn: cream

100% wool felt: cream

100% wool roving: cream

Pink seed bead

2 black glass eyes,
10 or 12 mm

Template: ears
(page 122)

Pink chalk

Sewing needle

White upholstery thread

6-inch (15.2 cm)
white pipe cleaner

Needle felting supplies
(page 16)

Ribbon

Millinery flowers

Tiny basket

FINISHED MEASUREMENTS
**5¾ inches (14.6 cm) tall at
the top of the head, 7½ inches
(19 cm) tall at the tip of
the longest ear**

1. Following steps 2–6 of Making Pompoms by Hand on pages 19–21, make a 2½-inch (6.4 cm) egg-shaped pompom from cream yarn for the head. I used approximately ⅓ skein of medium-weight Patons Classic Wool, which is approximately 69 yards (63 m).

2. On the narrow end of the egg shape, locate where you want the nose to be. Make a small part into the "fur," place a small drop of glue in the part, and insert a pink seed bead. Pinch the fibers around the glue and bead to secure it. Let dry.

3. Using the inverted triangle layout (see Positioning the Nose and Eyes on page 22), decide where you want the eyes to be. Make a part in the yarn, carefully squeeze in a pea-size drop of glue for each eye, and gently insert the wire end of each glass eye into the pompom. Let the glue dry.

4. Using the template on page 122, cut two ears out of the wool felt. Rub the inside of each ear with pink chalk and blend it in with your finger. Squeeze a bit of glue onto the bottom flat part of each ear shape and pinch the lower edge together to give it dimension. Repeat this for the second ear. Use clothespins or hemostats to hold the ear bases together as they dry.

5. After the ears have dried, make a small part on top of the head over each eye, squeeze a bit of glue into the pile, and insert the ears. Pinch the fibers around the ears to secure them, and let dry.

6. Following the instructions for Creating and Attaching Whiskers (page 22), thread a sewing needle with a 5-inch (12.7 cm) double strand of white upholstery thread. Tie a knot in the middle, place a tiny smidge of glue on the knot, and "sew" in the whiskers. Snip off any excess so the whiskers are even on both sides.

7. Make another slightly larger pompom from cream yarn and trim it into a pear-shaped pompom for the body, about 3¾ inches (9.5 cm) tall. I used approximately ½ skein of medium-weight Patons Classic Wool, which is approximately 105 yards (96 m). The narrow top will be the Bunny's neck, and the heavier, rounded end will be the bottom of the Bunny as it sits upright. To create the illusion of the seated Bunny's haunches and tummy, trim out a V shape from the front center bottom of the belly area.

8. Glue the pipe cleaner into the top half of the pompom body. Simply make a horizontal part deep into the wool at the top, squeeze in a dime-size dollop of glue, and place the pipe cleaner snugly down into it; pinch the fibers of the wool yarn to secure it. This will become the frame for the arms of the Bunny, which you will needle felt. (See Creating Appendages on page 24.)

9. Glue the finished head onto the body. To create a cute, inquisitive expression, tilt the head to one side. Squeeze a nickel-size dollop of glue at the top of the body pompom and position the head as desired. To keep the head from falling off before the glue sets up, use a long floral pin to hold it in place until dry. Remove the pin after the glue has set up.

10. After the glue has fully dried, bend the pipe cleaners into the desired position and trim each arm to approximately 2½ inches (6.4 cm). Bend down and tightly crimp the sharp cut ends of the pipe cleaners because they can poke through the needle-felted ends.

11. Needle felt the Bunny's feet by rolling a golf ball–size bit of roving into a cigarlike shape and start needle felting to compact it down (see Attaching Feet and Small Appendages on page 26). Once it is a tight, dense 3-inch (7.6 cm) cigar shape, cut it evenly in half to make the two feet.

12. At the bottom of the pear shape make two separate slits into the wool "fur" and glue the hind feet into the body. Let dry.

13. After the pipe cleaner and glue have set up, take a thick bacon-size strip of roving and wrap it tightly around the pipe cleaner arms. Use more roving near the upper arm and shoulder area and taper off at the end to form a tiny paw. Needle felt the roving tightly to make it compact around the pipe cleaner so it will not unravel (see Needle Felting Appendages on page 24).

14. For the tail, take a bit of roving and needle felt a marble-size ball. On the backside bottom of the Bunny, insert the glue bottle tip and squeeze in a bit of glue. Place the Bunny tail in the glue and pinch the wool fibers around to secure it. Let dry.

15. Embellish your Bunny with a ribbon, millinery flowers, and a little basket.

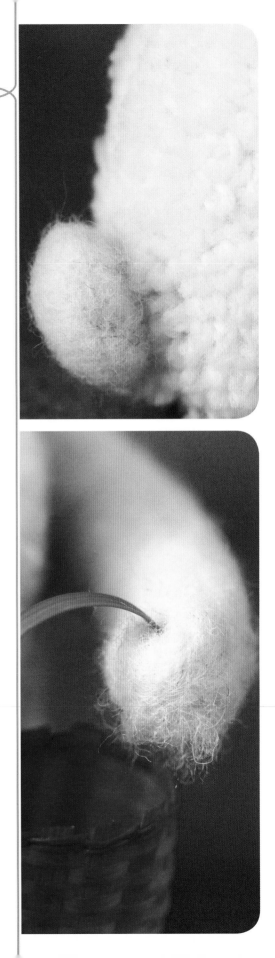

Mouse

This little Mouse is three parts charming, one part mischievous, and entirely filled with adventure: she's ready to journey down the river in her needle-felted leaf boat!

1. Following steps 2–6 of Making Pompoms by Hand on pages 19–21, make a 2½-inch (6.4 cm) egg-shaped pompom from gray yarn for the head. I used approximately ⅓ skein of Patons medium-weight Classic Wool, which is approximately 69 yards (63 m).

2. On the narrow end of the egg-shaped pompom, locate where you want the nose to be. Make a small part in the "fur," place a small drop of glue in the part, and insert the pink seed bead. Pinch the fibers around the glue and the bead to secure it. Let dry.

3. Using the inverted triangle layout (see Positioning the Nose and Eyes on page 22), decide where you want the eyes to be. Make a part in the yarn, carefully squeeze in a pea-size drop of glue for each eye, and gently insert the wire end of each glass eye into the pompom. Let the glue dry.

4. Using the template on page 121, cut two ears out of the wool felt. Rub the inside of each ear with pink chalk and blend it in with your finger. Squeeze a dollop of glue onto the bottom flat part of each ear shape and pinch the lower edge together, with the pink area inside, to give it dimension. Repeat this for the second ear. You can use clothespins or hemostats to hold the ear bases together as they dry.

5. After the ears have dried, make a small part on top of the head over each eye, squeeze a bit of glue into the pile, and insert the ears. Pinch the fibers around each ear to secure them and let dry.

6. Following the instructions for Creating and Attaching Whiskers (page 22), thread a sewing needle with a 5-inch (12.7 cm) double strand of white upholstery thread. Tie a knot in the center, place a tiny smidge of glue on the knot, and "sew" in the whiskers. Snip off any excess so the whiskers are even on both sides.

7. Make another slightly larger pompom by mixing gray yarn and cream yarn and trim it into a slightly pear-shaped pompom for the body, about 3¾ inches (9.5 cm) tall. I used approximately ⅓ skein of gray Patons medium-weight Classic Wool, which is approximately 69 yards (63 m), and approximately ¼ skein of cream Patons medium-weight Classic Wool, which is approximately 53 yds (48 m). The cream yarn will be the Mouse's tummy and the gray will be his

YOU WILL NEED

Basic Pompom Toolbox
(page 12)

100% wool yarn:
gray, cream

100% wool felt: gray

100% wool roving:
gray, green

Pink seed bead

2 black glass eyes, 10 or 12 mm

Template: ears (page 121)

Pink chalk

Sewing needle

White upholstery thread

2 pipe cleaners: 6-inch
(15.2 cm) gray and 10-inch
(25.4 cm) coordinating
color for the tail

Needle felting supplies
(page 16)

Ribbon

Millinery flowers

12 inches (30.5 cm) of
green fabric-covered
18-gauge floral wire

Velvet millinery leaf

FINISHED MEASUREMENTS
Mouse: 5¾ inches
(14.6 cm) tall
Leaf Boat: 5¼ inches
(13.3 cm) long from the leaf's
tip to the base of the stem

back and haunches. Using the heavier, fuller end of the pompom as the bottom, start shaping and trimming the pompom into a rounded pear shape. To create the definition of the Mouse's tummy and haunches, carefully trim out a V shape from the cream yarn on the center bottom of the belly area (see Shaping Pompoms page 29). Continue to trim the cream yarn down as necessary.

8. Glue the 6-inch (15.2 cm) pipe cleaner into the top half of the pompom body. Simply make a horizontal part deep into the wool at the top, squeeze in a dime-size dollop of glue, and place the pipe cleaner snugly down into it. Pinch the fibers of the wool yarn around the pipe cleaner to secure it. This will become the frame for the arms of the Mouse, which you will needle felt. (See Creating Appendages on page 24.)

9. Glue the finished head onto the body. To create a cute inquisitive expression, tilt the head to one side. Squeeze a nickel-size dollop of glue at the top of the body pompom and position the head as desired. To keep the head from falling off before the glue sets up, use a long floral pin to hold it in place. Remove the pin after the glue has set up.

10. After the glue has fully dried, bend the pipe cleaners into the desired position and trim each arm to approximately 2½ inches (6.4 cm). Bend down and tightly crimp the sharp cut ends of the pipe cleaners because they will poke through the needle-felted paws.

11. Needle felt the Mouse's feet by rolling a golf ball–size bit of gray roving into a cigarlike shape and start needle felting to compact it down. Once it is a tight, dense 3-inch (7.6 cm) cigar shape, cut it evenly in half to make the two feet.

12. At the bottom of the pear shape, make two separate parts into the wool "fur" and glue the feet into the body. Let it dry sitting upright.

13. After the pipe cleaner and glue have set up, take a thick bacon-size strip of roving and wrap it tightly around the pipe cleaner arms. Use more roving near the upper arm and shoulder area and taper off at the end to form a tiny paw. Needle felt the roving tightly to make it compact around the pipe cleaner so it will not unravel (see Needle Felting Appendages on page 24).

14. For the tail, trim the fuzzy fibers on one end of the 10-inch (25.4 cm) pipe cleaner with scissors to form a point. Shape the tail into a curled design. Squeeze a dollop of glue into the back bottom of your Mouse and insert the pipe cleaner. Squeeze the wool fibers around the tail to secure it. Let dry.

15. Embellish your Mouse with a ribbon and millinery flowers as desired.

16. To make the Leaf Boat, needle felt the green roving into a flat leaf shape. Add more roving as necessary and continue needle felting to bind the fibers together. Keep turning the leaf over and needle felt both sides until it becomes firm and dense and measures approximately 4 inches (10.2 cm) wide and 5 1/4 inches (13.3 cm) long. Mold the leaf into a shallow concave leaf shape that the Mouse can sit inside. Cut a 4-inch (10.2 cm) length of fabric-covered floral wire, coat one end with glue, and wedge it into the leaf to create a stem. Let the glue dry.

17. Cut a 7-inch (17.8 cm) length of fabric-covered floral wire and glue a velvet millinery leaf to one end to create a paddle for your Mouse to hold.

Kitten

Little kitties are sure to bring a smile to anyone's face! These instructions are for the Kitten sitting upright, but you can easily create a playful Kitten lying down by attaching the head toward the back of the shoulders, trimming the haunches more to the sides, and arranging the arms so they support the Kitten's body.

1. Following steps 2–6 of Making Pompoms by Hand on pages 19–21, make a 3-inch (7.6 cm) smooth, fat, egg-shaped pompom from white or cream yarn for the head. I used approximately ⅓ skein of Patons medium-weight Classic Wool, which is approximately 69 yards (63 m).

2. On the narrow end of the egg shape, locate where you want the nose to be. Make a small part into the "fur" of the yarn, squeeze in a small drop of glue, and insert a pink seed bead. Pinch the fibers around the glue and bead to secure it. Let dry.

3. Using the inverted triangle layout (see Positioning the Nose and Eyes on page 22), decide where you want the eyes to be. Make a part in the yarn, carefully squeeze in a pea-size drop of glue for each eye, and gently insert the wire end of each glass eye into the pompom. Let the glue dry.

4. Using the template on page 123, cut two ears out of the wool felt. Rub pink chalk inside each ear and blend it in with your finger.

5. Make a small part on top of the head over each eye and squeeze in a bit of glue. Insert the ears and pinch the fibers around the base of the ears to secure them; let dry.

6. Following the instructions for Creating and Attaching Whiskers (page 22), thread a sewing needle with a 5-inch (12.7 cm) double strand of white upholstery thread. Tie a knot in the middle, place a tiny smidge of glue on the knot, and "sew" in the whiskers. The knot should be approximately in the center front of the head. Snip off any excess so the whiskers are even on both sides.

7. Make another slightly larger pompom from white or cream yarn and trim it into a pear shape for the body, about 3¾ inches (9.5 cm) tall. I used approximately ½ skein of Patons medium-weight Classic Wool, which is approximately 105 yards (96 m). The narrow top will be the Kitten's neck and the heavier, rounded end will become the bottom of the Kitten as it sits upright. To create the illusion of the Kitten's haunches and tummy, trim out a V shape from the front center bottom of the belly area.

YOU WILL NEED

Basic Pompom Toolbox
(page 12)

100% wool yarn:
white or cream

100% wool felt:
white or cream

100% wool roving:
white or cream

Pink seed bead

2 black glass eyes, 10 or 12 mm

Template: ears (page 123)

Pink chalk

Sewing needle

White upholstery thread

2 white pipe cleaners,
6 inches (15.2 cm) and
8 inches (20.3 cm) long

Ribbon

Tiny bells

Millinery flowers

FINISHED MEASUREMENTS
6½ inches (16.5 cm) tall

Kitten

8. Glue the 6-inch (15.2 cm) pipe cleaner into the top half of the pompom body. Simply make a horizontal part deep into the wool at the top, squeeze in a dime-size dollop of glue, and place the pipe cleaner snugly down into it. Pinch the fibers of the wool yarn to secure it. This will become the frame for the arms of the Kitten, which you will needle felt. (See Creating Appendages on page 24.)

9. Glue the finished head onto the body. To create a cute, inquisitive expression, tilt the head to one side. Squeeze a nickel-size dollop of glue at the top of the body pompom and position the head as desired. You will need to let the glue set up and dry, which can take a while. To keep the head from falling off before the glue sets up, use a long floral pin to hold it in place. Remove the pin after the glue has set up.

10. After the pipe cleaner and glue have fully dried, bend the pipe cleaner into the desired position and trim each arm to approximately 3 inches (7.6 cm). Bend down and tightly crimp the sharp cut ends of the pipe cleaners because they can poke through and show out the end of the needle-felted paws.

11. Needle felt the Kitten's hind feet by rolling a golf ball–size bit of roving into a cigarlike shape and start needle felting to compact it down (see Attaching Feet and Small Appendages on page 26). Once it is a tight, dense 3-inch (7.6 cm) cigar shape, cut it evenly in half to make the two back paws.

12. At the bottom of the pear shape make two separate long slits into the wool "fur" and glue the feet into the body. Let it dry sitting upright.

13. After the pipe cleaner and glue have set up, take a thick bacon-size strip of roving and wrap it tightly from top to bottom around the pipe cleaner arms. Use more roving near the upper arm and shoulder area and taper off at the end to form a tiny paw. Needle felt the roving tightly to make it compact around the pipe cleaner so it will not unravel. Shave off excess "fuzzies" with scissors for a neater appearance, if desired (see Needle Felting Appendages on page 24).

14. For the tail, wrap wool roving tightly around the 8-inch (20.3 cm) pipe cleaner. Place a bit more roving toward one end, which will attach to the body, and let it taper off at the other end, which becomes the tip of the tail. Needle felt the entire tail evenly so the roving does not unravel. When finished, make a part at the bottom backside of the body pompom, squeeze in a small dollop of glue, and insert the tail. Gently pinch the wool fibers around it to secure the tail. Let dry. Curl the tail as desired.

15. Embellish your Kitten with little ribbons, tiny bells, and millinery flowers, if desired.

❋ **NOTE**: *There are other cute ideas for embellishments, too. Needle felt a little ball of yarn to place at the Kitten's feet or needle felt a tiny fish!*

❋ **VARIATION**: *To make a version of the Kitten lying down: attach the head pompom more toward the back of the body pompom; trim the haunches more to the sides of the body; and needle felt all four feet instead of using an armature for the front two.*

Bluebird

Bluebirds symbolize happiness and well-being: just take a look at this little gal's bright-eyed expression and you'll feel happy, too!

1. Following steps 2–6 of Making Pompoms by Hand on pages 19–21, make a 2½-inch (6.4 cm) round ball-shaped pompom from aqua yarn for the head. I used approximately ¼ skein of Patons medium-weight Classic Wool, which is approximately 53 yards (48 m).

2. Using the template on page 121 cut out a beak shape from orange or yellow wool felt.

3. Locate where you want the beak to be on the ball-shaped pompom. Make a small part into the pile of the yarn, place a drop of glue, and insert the wool felt beak. Pinch the fibers around the glue and wool felt beak to secure it. Let dry.

4. Using the inverted triangle layout (see Positioning the Nose and Eyes on page 22), decide where you want the eyes to be. Make a part in the yarn, carefully squeeze in a pea-size drop of glue for each eye, and gently insert the wire end of each glass eye into the pompom. Let the glue dry.

YOU WILL NEED

Basic Pompom Toolbox
(page 12)

100% wool yarn:
aqua blue

100% wool felt:
orange or yellow

Template: beak
(page 121)

2 black glass eyes,
10 or 12 mm

Wire cutters

32 inches (81.3 cm) of
18-gauge floral wire

Embroidery floss or
perle cotton: yellow or orange

Ribbon

Millinery flowers

FINISHED MEASUREMENTS
4 ¾ inches (12 cm) tall

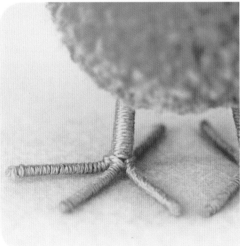

5. Make another slightly larger pompom from aqua blue yarn and trim it into an egg shape for the body, about 3½ inches (8.9 cm) from front to back and about 4 inches (10.2 cm) from top to bottom. Keep the yarn longer at the tail end and shape the back slightly. I used approximately ⅓ skein of Patons medium-weight Classic Wool, which is approximately 69 yards (63 m).

6. Glue the finished head onto the body. To create a cute, inquisitive expression, tilt the head to one side. Squeeze a nickel-size dollop of glue at the top of the body pompom and position the head as desired. You will need to let the glue set up and dry, which can take a few hours. To keep the head from falling off before the glue sets, use a long floral pin to hold it in place. Remove the pin after the glue has set up.

7. Using wire cutters, cut eight 4-inch (10.2 cm) pieces of floral wire.

8. To create each foot, take four pieces of wire, hold them together, and lightly coat the bundle with glue. Working from top to bottom, wind the embroidery floss or perle cotton tightly and uniformly around the wires. Stop approximately 1½ inches (3.8 cm) from reaching the bottom. Next, bend each wire out at a 90° angle to make individual toes. Three will face forward; one will face backward to provide the support needed for the Bluebird to stand. Continue wrapping each "toe" wire individually with embroidery floss to cover the floral wire. Repeat with the remaining four pieces of floral wire to create the other leg. Use wire cutters to snip off any excess wire length. Tuck any ends of embroidery floss underneath and let the glue dry.

9. At the bottom of the Bluebird's body, make two separate parts into the wool plush for the legs and squeeze a dollop of glue into each. Insert the wire legs and feet into the body. Pinch the wool fibers around the wrapped wire to secure. Set the Bluebird upright and make adjustments so that it can dry standing upright.

10. Embellish your Bluebird with a ribbon and millinery flowers.

✳ **NOTE:** *As another option in fashioning your Bluebird, purchase chicken feathers (different varieties are available) at your local craft store and use them, dyed to match the yarn, as the bird's tail instead. Simply make a part in the yarn, squeeze in a bit of glue, and insert the feathers.*

Elephant

They say Elephants have incredible memories—this little fellow's bright eyes
and friendly expression make him a creature you'll never forget.

Basic Pompom Toolbox
(page 12)

100% wool yarn:
gray

100% wool felt: gray, and
two colors of your choice

100% wool roving:
gray

4-inch (10.2 cm)
gray pipe cleaner

Needle felting supplies
(page 16)

2 black glass eyes,
10 or 12 mm

Template:
ears (page 122)

Wire cutters

12-inch (30.5 cm) length of
wooden dowel, 5 mm in diameter

Scallop-edge scissors or zigzag
pinking shears (optional)

Micro hole punch (optional)

Ribbon

FINISHED MEASUREMENTS
**5 ³⁄₄ inches (14.6 cm) tall
at the top of the head**

1. Following steps 2–6 of Making Pompoms by Hand on pages 19–21, make a 3-inch (7.6 cm) smooth, fat, egg-shaped pompom from gray yarn for the head. I used approximately ⅓ skein of Patons medium-weight Classic Wool, which is approximately 69 yards (63 m).

2. On the narrow end of the egg shape, locate where you want the nose to be and make a small part into the wool plush. Add glue and insert the pipe cleaner for the Elephant's trunk, curving it slightly. Pinch the fibers of the wool yarn around the pipe cleaner to secure it. Let dry.

3. Take a strip of gray wool roving, wrap it around the pipe cleaner tightly, and begin to needle felt the roving to the desired thickness for the Elephant's trunk (see Creating Appendages on page 24).

4. Using the inverted triangle layout (see Positioning the Nose and Eyes on page 22), decide where you want the eyes to be. Make a part in the yarn, carefully squeeze in a pea-size drop of glue for each eye, and gently insert the wire end of each glass eye into the pompom. Let the glue dry.

5. Using the template on page 122, cut two ears from the wool felt.

6. Make a small part in the wool on each side of the head and squeeze a bit of glue into the part; insert the ears. Pinch the fibers around the base of the ears to secure them, and let the glue dry.

7. Make another slightly larger pompom from the gray yarn and trim it into a fat bun-shaped pompom for the body measuring approximately 4 inches (10.2 cm) in length and diameter. I used approximately ½ skein of medium-weight Patons Classic Wool, which is approximately 105 yards (96 m).

8. To create the Elephant's legs, use your wire cutters and cut four equal pieces from the wooden dowel to create legs approximately 3 inches (7.6 cm) long.

9. Wrap each leg thickly with strips of wool roving and begin to needle felt around the dowel (see Needle Felting Appendages on page 24). Needle felt the roving tightly and evenly around the legs. Be sure to needle felt over the bottom of the dowel so it is not exposed. Shave off any excess "fuzzies" with your scissors for a neater appearance, if desired.

10. Make four deep parts on the bottom of the Elephant's body where you want to position the legs. Add glue in each part and insert the legs, firmly pinching the wool fibers around the legs to secure them. Adjust the legs as necessary so the Elephant can stand. Let it dry standing upright.

11. Glue the finished head onto the body. To create a cute, inquisitive expression, tilt the head to one side. Squeeze a nickel-size dollop of glue at the top of the body pompom and position the head as desired. You will need to let the glue set up and dry, which can take a while. To keep the head from falling off before the glue sets up, use a long floral pin to hold it in place. Remove the pin after the glue has set up and dried.

12. For the tail, cut nine pieces of gray yarn into 6-inch (15.2 cm) lengths and tightly knot them together at one end. Divide the yarn into three sections, each with three pieces of yarn, and braid the three sections together. Knot the end and even it off with scissors. Make a part in the pompom body where you want to insert the tail, squeeze in a small dollop of glue, and insert the tail. Gently pinch the wool fibers around to secure the tail. Let dry.

13. Using the scallop-edge scissors or pinking shears if possible, cut an oval from each color of felt, one measuring 3 inches (7.6 cm) long and the other 2 1/2 inches (6.4 cm) long. Decorate the edges of the ovals with a micro hole punch, if desired. Glue the smaller oval onto the larger one, then glue both onto the back of the Elephant, using a pipe cleaner or ribbon to hold them in place while the glue dries.

14. Embellish your Elephant with a ribbon.

❋ **NOTE:** *Other ideas for embellishments include tiny bells, millinery flowers, and/or the top hat described on page 115.*

Lop-Eared Bunny

With bashful lop ears and an armful of springtime flowers,
this sweet bunny is ready to hippity-hop into your heart.

1. Following steps 2–6 of Making Pompoms by Hand on pages 19–21, make a 2½- to 3-inch (6.4 to 7.6 cm) egg-shaped pompom from white or cream yarn for the head. I used approximately ⅓ skein of Patons medium-weight Classic Wool, which is approximately 69 yards (63 m).

2. On the narrow end of the egg-shaped pompom, locate where you want the nose to be. Make a small part into the "fur," place a small drop of glue in the part, and insert the pink seed bead. Pinch the fibers around the glue and the bead to secure it. Let dry.

3. Using the inverted triangle layout (see Positioning the Nose and Eyes on page 22), decide where you want the eyes to be. Make a part in the yarn, carefully squeeze in a pea-size drop of glue for each eye, and gently insert the wire end of each glass eye into the pompom. Let the glue dry.

4. Using the template on page 124, cut two ears from the black wool felt. Using the template as a guide, use a flat iron or a regular household iron to create a folded edge at the base of the Bunny's ears so they will flop over.

5. Make a small part on top of the head over each eye, squeeze a bit of glue into the parted pile, and insert the ears. Pinch the fibers around the ears to secure them and let the glue dry.

6. Following the instructions for Creating and Attaching Whiskers (page 22), thread a sewing needle with a 5-inch (12.7 cm) double strand of white upholstery thread. Tie a knot in the center, place a tiny smidge of glue on the knot, and "sew" in the whiskers. Snip off any excess so the whiskers are even on both sides.

7. Make another slightly larger pompom from white or cream yarn and trim it into a pear-shaped pompom for the body, about 4 inches (10.2 cm) tall. I used approximately ½ skein of Patons medium-weight Classic Wool, which is approximately 105 yards (96 m). The narrow top will be the Bunny's neck, and the heavier, rounded end will be the bottom of the Bunny as it sits upright. To create the illusion of the Bunny's haunches and tummy, trim out a V shape from the front center bottom of the belly area.

YOU WILL NEED

Basic Pompom Toolbox
(page 12)

100% wool yarn:
white or cream

100% wool felt: black

100% wool roving:
white or cream, and black

Pink seed bead

2 black glass eyes,
10 or 12 mm

Template:
ears (page 124)

Hair-straightening flat iron
or household iron

Sewing needle

White upholstery thread

6-inch (15.2 cm)
white pipe cleaner

Needle felting supplies
(page 16)

Ribbon

Millinery flowers

FINISHED MEASUREMENTS
6 inches (15.2 cm) tall

Lop-Eared Bunny

8. Glue the pipe cleaner into the top half of the pompom body. Simply make a horizontal part deep into the wool at the top, squeeze in a dime-size dollop of glue, and place the pipe cleaner snugly down into it. Pinch the fibers of the wool yarn to secure the pipe cleaner. This will become the frame for the arms of the Bunny, which you will needle felt. (See Creating Appendages on page 24.)

9. Glue the finished head onto the body. Squeeze a nickel-size dollop of glue at the top of the body pompom and position the head as desired. To keep the head from falling off before the glue sets up, use a long floral pin to hold it in place. Remove the pin after the glue has set up and dried.

10. After the glue has fully dried, bend the pipe cleaners into the desired position and trim each arm to approximately 2½ inches (6.4 cm). Bend down and tightly crimp the sharp cut ends of the pipe cleaners because they will poke through the needle-felted ends.

11. Needle felt the Bunny's feet by rolling a golf ball–size bit of white or cream roving into a cigarlike shape and start needle felting to compact it down (see Attaching Feet and Small Appendages on page 26). Once it is a tight, dense 3-inch (7.6 cm) cigar shape, cut it evenly in half to make the two feet.

12. At the bottom of the pear shape make two separate slits into the wool "fur" and glue the hind feet into the body. Let it dry sitting upright.

13. After the pipe cleaner and glue have set up, take a thick bacon-size strip of roving and wrap it tightly around the pipe cleaner arms. Use more roving near the upper arm and shoulder area and taper off at the end to form a tiny paw. Needle felt the roving tightly to compact it around the pipe cleaner so it will not unravel (see Needle Felting Appendages on page 24).

14. For the tail, take a bit of black roving and needle felt a marble-size ball. On the backside bottom of the Bunny, insert the glue bottle and squeeze in a bit of glue. Place the Bunny tail in and pinch the wool fibers around to secure it. Let dry.

15. Embellish your Bunny with a ribbon and millinery flowers.

Ladybug

Ladybugs are said to bring good luck. With her sweetly curled antennae and clever felt feet, the recipient of this project will be lucky, indeed. The Ladybug's red and black body pompom is made by layering the two colors of yarn: three sections of wrapped black yarn become six black spots on this pretty lady's back.

Basic Pompom Toolbox
(page 12)

100% wool yarn:
black, red

100% wool felt:
black

2 black glass eyes,
10 or 12 mm

8-inch (20.3 cm)
black pipe cleaner

Template:
feet (page 123)

Ribbon

Millinery flowers

FINISHED MEASUREMENTS
5 inches (12.7 cm) long from
front to back;
2½ inches (6.4 cm) tall at
the top of the back

1. Following steps 2–6 of Making Pompoms by Hand on pages 19–21, make a 1¾-inch (4.4 cm) round, ball-shaped pompom from black yarn for the head. I used approximately ¼ skein of Patons medium-weight Classic Wool, which is approximately 53 yards (48 m).

2. Using the inverted triangle layout (see Positioning the Nose and Eyes on page 22), decide where you want the eyes to be. Make a part in the yarn, carefully squeeze in a pea-size drop of glue for each eye, and gently insert the wire end of each glass eye into the pompom. Let the glue dry.

3. Cut two 3-inch (7.6 cm) lengths of the black pipe cleaner to create the Ladybug's antennae. On one end of each pipe cleaner curl the ends into a spiral. You can do this by hand or by winding the pipe cleaner around a pencil. Make a tiny part on the top of the head above each eye. Insert the tip of the glue bottle and squeeze in a tiny dollop of glue. Insert the uncurled end of each pipe cleaner into the head at this spot and pinch the fibers around it to secure the antennae. Let dry.

4. The Ladybug's body pompom is made a bit differently than other multicolor pompoms in this book. Instead of only winding different colors of yarn side-by-side, this black and red pompom is made by winding multicolor layers of yarn on top of each other. Overall, I used a total of approximately ¼ skein of red Patons medium-weight Classic Wool, which is approximately 53 yards (48 m), and a total of approximately ⅛ skein of black Classic Wool for the spots, which is approximately 26 yards (24 m).

5. Your goal will be to make the black spots roughly the same size, which means you'll want to use about the same amount of black yarn each time you wind it on the cardboard sleeve. When I want to keep relatively small amounts of yarn equal in size, I find it helpful to count my number of wraps. You can also pre-cut the shorter lengths of yarn used in the second and third layers.

✳ **NOTE**: *Think of this pompom as being made from four layers of yarn. The three sections of wrapped black yarn will eventually become the Ladybug's six black spots.*

LAYER 1 Wrap approximately one third of the red yarn around the cardboard sleeve, about 18 yards (16 m).

LAYER 2 On top of the first all-red layer, wrap a sequence of black-red-black yarn: wrap about 9 yards (8 m) of black on the left; about 6 yards (5 m) of red in the center; and about 9 yards (8 m) of black on the right.

LAYER 3 On top of the first and second layers, wrap a reverse sequence of red-black-red yarn: wrap about 6 yards (5 m) of red on the left; about 9 yards (8 m) of black in the center; and about 6 yards (5 m) of red on the right.

LAYER 4 On top of the first, second, and third layers, wrap another all-red layer of yarn, about 18 yards (16 m).

6. Slide the four-layer bundle of yarn off the cardboard sleeve, tie it with waxed twine, and cut the pompom's loops as described in Steps 3-5 of Making Pompoms by Hand (pages 19–21).

7. The flat bottom of the Ladybug's body pompom is created by pressing all the yarn fibers upward by hand so a flattened side naturally forms—don't cut the fibers. Once you cut the loops of the pompom, you'll see six areas of black yarn that will form the Ladybug's spots. Comb and gently tug the yarn fibers with your fingers to arrange the black sections of yarn into evenly-spaced spots surrounded by red yarn.

8. When you've arranged the black and red yarn, trim and sculpt the pompom into a hemisphere or dome measuring approximately 4 1/2 inches (11.4 cm) in length. The flattened side of the pompom will become the Ladybug's underbelly.

9. Glue the finished head onto the body by squeezing a dollop of glue at the top of the body pompom and positioning the head as desired. To keep the head from falling off before the glue sets up, use a long floral pin to hold it in place. Remove the pin after the glue has dried.

10. Using the template on page 123, cut out six feet from black wool felt.

11. Glue the feet onto the bottom of the body pompom as shown, with three feet on each side.

12. Add ribbon and floral embellishments, as desired, to your little Ladybug.

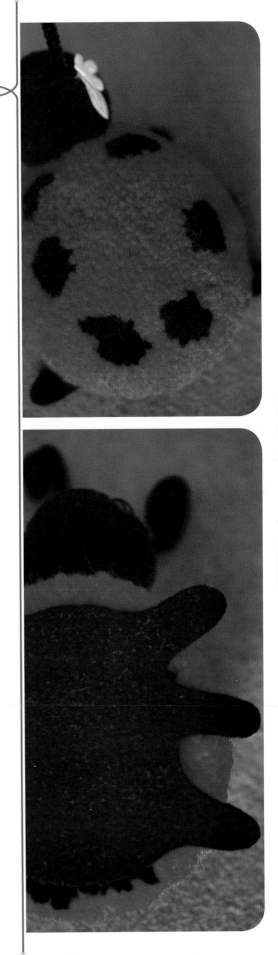

Teddy Bear

Teddy bears embody the classic toy and youthful companion throughout the ages.
Create your own heirloom bear using the techniques described here, or use a few
simple adjustments to transform your bear into a Panda.

1. Following steps 2–6 of Making Pompoms by Hand on pages 19–21, make a 3-inch (7.6 cm) smooth, fat, egg-shaped pompom from gray yarn for the head. I used approximately ⅓ skein of Patons medium-weight Classic Wool, which is approximately 69 yards (63 m). Sculpt a muzzle for the Teddy Bear's face (see Tips on Shaping the Nose and Muzzle, page 21).

2. On the muzzle, locate where you want the nose to be. Make a small part into the "fur," place a small drop of glue in the part, and insert the black seed bead. Pinch the fibers around the glue and the bead to secure it. Let the glue dry.

3. Using the inverted triangle layout (see Positioning the Nose and Eyes on page 22), decide where you want the eyes to be. Make a part in the yarn, carefully squeeze in a pea-size drop of glue for each eye, and gently insert the wire end of each glass eye into the pompom. Let the glue dry.

4. Using the template on page 123, cut two ears out of the wool felt. Place glue on the bottom flat part of the ear shape and pinch the lower edge together to create dimension. Repeat this for the second ear. Use clothespins or hemostats to hold the ear bases together as they dry.

5. Make a small part on the top of the head above each eye, squeeze a bit of glue into the part, and insert the ears. Pinch the fibers around the base of the ears to secure them and let the glue dry.

YOU WILL NEED

Basic Pompom Toolbox
(page 12)

100% wool yarn:
gray

100% wool felt:
gray

100% wool roving:
gray

Black seed bead

2 black glass eyes,
10 or 12 mm

Template:
ears (page 123)

Two 7-inch (17.8 cm)
gray pipe cleaners

Needle felting supplies
(page 16)

Ribbon

FINISHED MEASUREMENTS
**Teddy Bear:
5 ¾ inches (14.6 cm) tall**

Teddy Bear

✻ VARIATION: *Use a few simple adjustments to transform your Teddy Bear into a Panda: use white or cream yarn for the body and head, black felt for the ears, and black roving for the arms. For the Panda, you can attach needle-felted black feet to the body pompom instead of making the legs from a needle-felted pipe cleaner.*

Teddy Bear

6. Make another slightly larger pompom from the gray yarn and trim it into a pear-shaped pompom for the body, about 4 inches (10.2 cm) in length and diameter. I used approximately ½ skein of Patons medium-weight Classic Wool, which is approximately 105 yards (96 m). Using your scissors, sculpt a fat little belly for the Teddy Bear.

7. To create the gray Teddy Bear's arms and legs, make a deep part at the top of the pear shape of the body and glue in a pipe cleaner approximately 7 inches (17.8 cm) in length, with even parts sticking out on each side for the arms. Repeat with another pipe cleaner in the pompom's heavier bottom end for the legs. Pinch the fibers around the glue and pipe cleaners to secure them. These will become the frames for the legs, which you will needle felt. (See Creating Appendages on page 24.) Let the glue dry.

8. Trim the pipe cleaners to approximately 3½ inches (8.9 cm) long for each of the arms and legs. Fold down and crimp any sharp edges of the pipe cleaners because they can poke out of the needle-felted paws.

9. Bend the bottom pipe cleaners so the Teddy Bear is sitting with his bottom legs sticking out in front.

10. Wrap each pipe cleaner appendage thickly and firmly in wool roving and needle felt around each of the pipe cleaners. Needle felt the roving tightly, making the top ends slightly thicker than the bottoms of the leg (see Needle Felting Appendages on page 24). Add more roving to the Teddy Bear's feet to create and shape toes.

11. Glue the finished head onto the body. To create a cute, inquisitive expression, tilt the head to one side. Squeeze a nickel-size dollop of glue at the top of the body pompom and position the head as desired. You will need to let the glue set up and dry, which can take a while. To keep the head from falling off before the glue sets up, use a long floral pin to hold it in place. Remove the pin after the glue has set up.

12. For the tail, needle felt a bit of roving into a flattened, pea-size oval. Make a part at the bottom backside, squeeze in a small dollop of glue, and insert the tail. Gently pinch the wool fibers around the tail to secure it. Let dry.

13. Tie a ribbon around your Teddy Bear's neck.

Lamb

Little lambs are a sweet sign of spring and new life, making this project a wonderful gift to give when the days grow warmer and spring is in the air.

Basic Pompom Toolbox
(page 12)

100% wool yarn:
white or cream

100% wool felt:
white or cream

100% wool roving yarn:
white or cream

100% wool roving:
white or cream

2 black glass eyes,
10 or 12 mm

Template:
ears (page 121)

Pink chalk

Wire cutters

12-inch (30.5 cm)
length of wooden dowel,
5 mm in diameter

Needle felting supplies
(see page 16)

Ribbon

Tiny bells

Millinery flowers

FINISHED MEASUREMENTS
6 inches (15.2 cm) tall

1. Following steps 2–6 of Making Pompoms by Hand on pages 19–21, make a 3-inch (7.6 cm) smooth, fat, egg-shaped pompom from white yarn for the head. I used approximately ⅓ skein of Patons medium-weight Classic Wool, which is approximately 69 yards (63 m).

2. Using the inverted triangle layout (see Positioning the Nose and Eyes on page 22), decide where you want the eyes to be. Make a part in the yarn, carefully squeeze in a pea-size drop of glue for each eye, and gently insert the wire end of each glass eye into the pompom. Let the glue dry. The Lamb has no nose.

3. Using the template on page 121, cut two ears out of the wool felt. Rub pink chalk inside each ear and blend it in with your finger. Squeeze a dollop of glue onto the bottom flat part of each ear shape and pinch the lower edge together, with the pink area inside, to give it dimension. Repeat this for the second ear. You can use clothespins or hemostats to hold the ear bases together as they dry.

4. Make a small part on each side of the head, squeeze a bit of glue into the part, and insert the ears. Pinch the fibers around the base of the ears to secure them and let the glue dry.

5. Make another slightly larger pompom from white roving yarn and trim it into a fat bun-shaped pompom for the body, measuring about 4 inches (10.2 cm) in length and diameter. I used approximately ⅓ skein of Patons bulky-weight Classic Wool Roving yarn, which is approximately 40 yards (36 m).

6. To create the Lamb's legs, use your wire cutters to cut four equal pieces of the wooden dowel to create legs approximately 3 inches (7.6 cm) long.

7. Wrap each leg thickly in wool roving and needle felt around the dowel (see Needle Felting Appendages on page 24). Needle felt the roving tightly, making the top of the leg near the body slightly thicker than the bottom. Be sure to needle felt over the bottom of the dowel so it is not exposed. Shave off any excess "fuzzies" with scissors for a neater appearance, if desired.

8. Make four deep parts on the bottom of the Lamb's body where you want to position the legs. Add glue in each part and insert the legs, firmly pinching the wool fibers around the legs to secure them. Adjust the legs as necessary so the Lamb can stand. Let it dry standing upright.

9. Glue the finished head onto the body. To create a cute, inquisitive expression, tilt the head to one side. Squeeze a nickel-size dollop of glue at the top of the body pompom and position the head as desired. You will need to let the glue set up and dry, which can take a while. To keep the head from falling off before the glue sets up, use a long floral pin to hold it in place. Remove the pin after the glue has set up and dried.

10. For the tail, take a bit of roving and needle felt a flattened marble-size oval shape. Make a part at the bottom backside, squeeze in a small dollop of glue, and gently insert the tail. Pinch the wool fibers around the tail to secure it. Let dry.

11. Embellish your Lamb with ribbons, tiny bells, and millinery flowers, as desired.

Puppy

Say hello to a crafter's best friend: this wiggly, waggy, playful pompom pup.

YOU WILL NEED

Basic Pompom Toolbox
(page 12)

100% wool yarn:
gray

100% wool felt:
gray

100% wool roving:
gray

Black seed bead

2 black glass eyes,
10 or 12 mm

Template:
ears (page 121)

Hair-straightening flat iron
or household iron

Sewing needle

Black upholstery thread

Two 6-inch (15.2 cm)
pipe cleaners

Needle felting supplies
(page 16)

Narrow ribbon

Tiny bell

FINISHED MEASUREMENTS
6 1/4 inches (15.9 cm) tall

1. Following steps 2–6 for Making Pompoms by Hand on pages 19–21, make a 3-inch (7.6 cm) smooth, fat, egg-shaped pompom from gray yarn for the head. I used approximately 1/3 skein of Patons medium-weight Classic Wool, which is approximately 69 yards (63 m). Scupt a muzzle for the Puppy's face (see Tips on Shaping the Nose and Muzzle, page 21).

2. On the muzzle, locate where you want the nose to be. Make a small part into the "fur," place a small drop of glue, and insert the black seed bead. Pinch the fibers around the glue and the bead to secure it.

3. Using the inverted triangle layout (see Positioning the Nose and Eyes on page 22), decide where you want the eyes to be. Make a part in the yarn, carefully squeeze in a pea-size drop of glue for each eye, and gently insert the wire end of each glass eye into the pompom. Let the glue dry.

4. Using the template on page 121, cut two ears out of the wool felt. With the template as a guide, use a flat iron or household iron to create a crease in the Puppy's ears so they will flop over.

5. Make a small part on top of the head over each eye and squeeze a bit of glue into the part in the wool fibers; insert the ears. Pinch the fibers around the base of the ears to secure them and let the glue dry.

6. Following the instructions for Creating and Attaching Whiskers (page 22), thread a sewing needle with a 5-inch (12.7 cm) double strand of black upholstery thread. Tie a knot in the middle, place a tiny smidge of glue on the knot, and "sew" in the whiskers; the knot should be in the approximate center front of the head. Snip off any excess so the whiskers are even on both sides.

7. Make another slightly larger pompom from gray yarn and trim it into a pear-shaped pompom for the body, about 4 inches (10.2 cm) tall. I used approximately ½ skein of Patons medium-weight Classic Wool, which is approximately 105 yards (96 m). The narrow top will be the Puppy's neck, and the heavier, rounded end will become the bottom of the Puppy as it sits upright. To create the illusion of the Puppy's haunches and tummy, trim out a V shape from the front center bottom of the belly area.

8. Glue a 6-inch (15.2 cm) pipe cleaner into the top half of the pompom body. Simply make a horizontal part deep into the wool at the top, squeeze in a dime-size dollop of glue, and place the pipe cleaner snugly down into it. Pinch the fibers of the wool yarn around the pipe cleaner to secure it. This will become the frame for the arms of the Puppy, which you will needle felt. (See Creating Appendages on page 24.)

9. Glue the finished head onto the body. To create a cute, inquisitive expression, tilt the head to one side. Squeeze a nickel-size dollop of glue at the top of the body pompom and position the head as desired. You will need to let the glue set up and dry, which can take a while. To keep the head from falling off before the glue sets up, use a long floral pin to hold it in place. Remove the pin after the glue has set up.

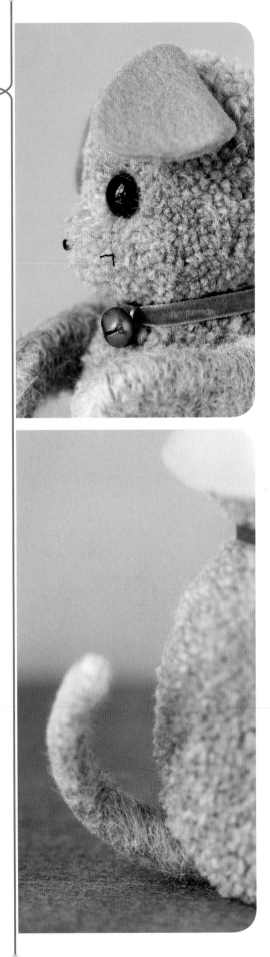

10. After the glue has fully dried, bend the pipe cleaner into the desired position and trim the arms to approximately 3 inches (7.6 cm). Bend down and tightly crimp the sharp cut ends of the pipe cleaners because they can poke through and show out the end of the needle-felted paws.

11. Needle felt the Puppy's hind feet by rolling a golf ball–size bit of roving into a cigarlike shape and start needle felting to compact it down (see Attaching Feet and Small Appendages on page 26). Once it is a tight, dense 3-inch (7.6 cm) cigar shape, cut it evenly in half to make the two back paws.

12. At the bottom of the pear shape make two separate long slits into the wool "fur" and glue the feet into the body. Let it dry sitting upright.

13. After the pipe cleaner and glue have set up, take a thick bacon-size strip of roving and wrap it tightly from top to bottom around the pipe cleaner arms. Use more roving near the upper arm and shoulder area and taper off at the end to form a paw. Needle felt the roving tightly to compact it around the pipe cleaner so it will not unravel. Shave off any excess "fuzzies" with your scissors for a neater appearance, if desired.

14. For the tail, cut a pipe cleaner approximately 5¼ inches (13.3 cm) long and wrap roving tightly around it from top to bottom. Place a bit more roving toward the end that will attach to the body and taper it off at the tip of the tail. Needle felt the entire tail evenly so the roving does not unravel. When finished, make a part at the bottom backside of the Puppy, squeeze in a small dollop of glue, and gently insert the tail. Gently pinch the wool fibers around the tail to secure it. Let dry.

15. Embellish your Puppy with a narrow ribbon "collar" strung with a tiny bell.

❀ **NOTE**: *For other cute accessories for your Puppy, needle felt a bone or a dog dish.*

Swan

No other bird is as graceful or as beautiful as a swan. These make great gifts as love tokens—swans (like many birds) symbolize eternal love because they mate for life.

Basic Pompom Toolbox
(page 12)

100% wool roving yarn:
white

100% wool roving:
white, orange, black

Wire cutters

7 inches (17.8 cm) of
18-gauge floral wire

Needle felting supplies
(page 16)

2 black glass eyes,
8 mm

FINISHED MEASUREMENTS
4 1/4 inches (10.8 cm)
tall at the top arch of the neck;
3 1/4 inches (8.3 cm)
tall at the top of the back

1. Following steps 2–6 of Making Pompoms by Hand on pages 19–21, make a 4 x 5-inch (10.2 x 12.7 cm) tear-shaped oval pompom from white roving yarn for the body. I used approximately 1/3 skein of Patons bulky-weight Classic Wool Roving, which is approximately 40 yards (36 m). Wool roving yarn is much fluffier than regular wool yarn and will create beautiful feathers on the Swan. The pointed end of the pompom will be the Swan's tail. Flatten the bottom so the pompom sits level and flush.

2. Using your wire cutters, cut a 6- to 7-inch length of 18-gauge floral wire and fold it in half. Bend the doubled wire into a graceful S-curve that will be the frame of the needle-felted head and neck. Use wire cutters to trim the neck length accordingly.

3. Thickly wrap the neck armature with white wool roving, concentrating more roving on the folded end, which will become the Swan's head. Begin needle felting to keep the roving from unraveling (see Creating Appendages, page 24).

Swan

4. Continue needle felting, adding more roving as necessary, building up and making a slightly rounded end over the folded wire. Needle felt this into a marble-size head, about 1 inch (2.5 cm) long, compacting the roving around the head and neck tightly and evenly.

5. Make the beak by shaping and needle felting a bit of orange roving into a slim, pointy triangle about ½ inch (1.3 cm) long. Remember to needle felt the beak from multiple angles, creating a dense shape. Attach the beak by needle felting it directly onto the white roving of the head.

6. Decide where to place the eyes on each side of the Swan's head. Use a pencil to poke a hole into the roving on each side of the head to create an indentation, insert the tip of the glue bottle, and squeeze in a tiny bit of glue. Place a glass eye into each drop of glue and gently push it in. Let the glue dry.

7. Needle felt a bit of black roving around the beak and each eye to create detail for the Swan's face.

8. Make a part in the rounded end of the pompom body and squeeze in a large dollop of glue. Insert the needle-felted neck and head. Pinch the wool fibers around the neck to secure it. Let dry.

Seal

Seals are known for their playfulness: now, instead of only getting to see them play at the zoo or circus, you can create one to look at all year long! Try your hand at a white or spotted seal as a friend for this gray fellow.

1. Following steps 2–6 of Making Pompoms by Hand on pages 19–21, make a 2½-inch (6.4 cm) egg-shaped pompom from gray yarn for the head. I used approximately ⅓ skein of Patons medium-weight Classic Wool, which is approximately 69 yards (63 m).

2. On the narrow end of the egg shape, locate where you want the nose to be. Make a small part into the "fur," place a small drop of glue, and insert a black seed bead. Pinch the fibers around the glue and the bead to secure it.

3. Using the inverted triangle layout (see Positioning the Nose and Eyes on page 22), decide where you want the eyes to be. Make a part in the yarn, carefully squeeze in a pea-size drop of glue for each eye, and gently insert the wire end of each glass eye into the pompom. Let the glue dry.

4. Following the instructions for Creating and Attaching Whiskers (page 22), thread a sewing needle with a 5-inch (12.7 cm) double strand of black upholstery thread. Tie a knot in the center, place a tiny smidge of glue on the knot, and "sew" in the whiskers. Snip off any excess so the whiskers are even on both sides.

YOU WILL NEED

Basic Pompom Toolbox
(page 12)

100% wool yarn:
gray

100% wool felt:
gray

100% wool roving:
color of your choice for the ball

Black seed bead

2 black glass eyes,
10 or 12 mm

Sewing needle

Black upholstery thread

Templates:
flippers, tail
(page 124)

Needle felting supplies
(page 16)

Pipe cleaner

Ribbon

FINISHED MEASUREMENTS
**4½ inches (11.4 cm) tall
at the tip of the nose,
4¼ inches (10.8 cm) long
without the felt tail**

Seal

5. Make another slightly large pompom from gray yarn and trim it into an oblong, tear-shaped pompom for the body, about 4 inches (10.2 cm) long. I used approximately ½ skein of Patons medium-weight Classic Wool, which is approximately 105 yards (96 m). The heavier, rounded end will be the Seal's upper chest and neck. The narrow end will taper off to the Seal's tail. Trim the bottom of the pompom flat so the Seal can lie on its belly.

6. Using the template on page 124, cut two flippers from the wool felt. Make a part in the wool yarn fur on each side of the front end of the body pompom at a slight diagonal, squeeze glue into the part, and insert a flipper on each side. Pinch the fibers around each flipper to secure them and let dry.

7. Using the template on page 124, cut out the tail flipper from the wool felt. Make a horizontal part at the end of the tail, squeeze some glue into the part, and insert the tail flipper. Pinch the fibers around the tail to secure it and let dry.

8. Glue the finished head onto the body with the Seal's nose pointing straight up. Squeeze a nickel-size dollop of glue at the top of the body pompom and position the head as desired. To keep the head from falling off before the glue sets up, use a long floral pin to hold it in place. Remove the pin after the glue has set up and dried.

9. Using a roving color of your choice, needle felt a ball for the Seal to balance on its nose. Roll a small bit of roving into a ball and needle felt into a dense, smooth, round shape about ¾ inch (1.9 cm) in diameter. Don't make the ball too large or it will be too heavy for the Seal to "balance" on its nose. Trim any loose "fuzzies" to make the ball neater.

10. Make a tiny snip in the needle-felted ball. Cut a ¾-inch (1.9 cm) length of pipe cleaner, dip one end into the glue, and insert it into the ball halfway. Let dry.

11. Make a tiny part as close to the Seal's nose as you can and squeeze in a bit of glue. Insert the pipe cleaner from the needle-felted ball into the part and pinch the yarn fibers around the pipe cleaner to secure it. Allow the glue to dry completely. Now your Seal is balancing a ball on the end of his nose!

12. Tie a ribbon around your Seal's neck.

Piglet

That little piggy went to market, and this little piggy stayed home to be with you!

Basic Pompom Toolbox
(page 12)

100% wool yarn:
pink

100% wool felt:
pink

100% wool roving:
pink

Embroidery needle

Embroidery floss:
pink

2 black glass eyes,
10 or 12 mm

Template:
ears (page 121)

Hair-straightening flat iron
or household iron

Two 6-inch (15.2 cm)
pink pipe cleaners

Needle felting supplies
(page 16)

Ribbon

FINISHED MEASUREMENTS
5½ inches (14 cm) tall

1. Following steps 2–6 of Making Pompoms by Hand on pages 19–21, make a 3-inch (7.6 cm) smooth, fat, egg-shaped pompom from pink yarn for the head. I used approximately ⅓ skein of Patons medium-weight Classic Wool, which is approximately 69 yards (63 m).

2. Because the narrower end of the pompom head will become the Piglet's nose, after shaping the head and snout (see Tips on Shaping the Nose and Muzzle, page 21), trim the snout's end flat.

3. Take a bit of pink wool felt and cut an oval about ¾ x ½ inch (1.9 x 1.3 cm). Embroider two little nostrils using French knots or simple straight stitches with the pink embroidery floss. Glue the little oval onto the end of the nose to make the Piglet's snout.

4. Using the inverted triangle layout (see Positioning the Nose and Eyes on page 22), decide where you want the eyes to be. Make a part in the yarn, carefully squeeze in a pea-size drop of glue for each eye, and gently insert the wire end of each glass eye into the pompom. Let the glue dry.

5. Using the template on page 121, cut two ears from the pink wool felt. With the template as a guide, use a flat iron or household iron to create a crease at the base of the Piglet's ears so they will flop over.

6. Make a small part on each side of the head, squeeze a bit of glue into each part in the wool fibers, and insert the ears. Pinch the fibers around the base of the ears to secure them and let the glue dry.

7. Make another slightly larger pompom from pink yarn and trim it into a pear-shaped pompom for the body, measuring approximately 4 inches (10.2 cm) in length and diameter. I used

approximately ½ skein of Patons medium-weight Classic Wool, which is approximately 105 yards (96 m). To create the illusion of the Piglet's tummy and haunches as it sits, trim out a V shape from the front center bottom of the belly area.

8. Glue a pipe cleaner into the top half of the pompom body. Simply make a horizontal part deep into the wool at the top, squeeze in a dime-size dollop of glue, and place the pipe cleaner snugly down into it. Pinch the fibers of the wool yarn around the pipe cleaner to secure it. This will become the frame for the arms of the Piglet, which you will needle felt. (See Creating Appendages on page 24.)

9. After the pipe cleaner and glue have set up, take a thick bacon-size strip of pink roving and wrap it tightly around each pipe cleaner arm. Use more roving near the upper arm and shoulder area and taper off at the end to form a tiny hoof. Needle felt the roving tightly to compact it around the pipe cleaner so it will not unravel (see Needle Felting Appendages on page 24).

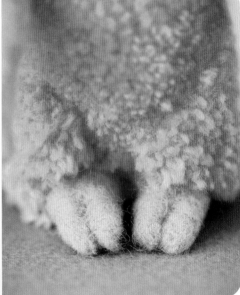

10. Needle felt the Piglet's feet by rolling a golf ball–size bit of pink roving into a cigarlike shape and continue needle felting to compact it down. Once it is a tight, dense 3-inch (7.6 cm) cigar shape, cut it evenly in half to make the two feet.

11. Take your scissors and vertically snip the ends of all four appendages to create the cloven hooves on the Piglet. Continue to needle felt the loose roving ends and shape them into hooves.

12. Glue the finished head onto the body. To create a cute, inquisitive expression, tilt the head to one side. Squeeze a nickel-size dollop of glue at the top of the body pompom and position the head as desired. You will need to let the glue set up and dry, which can take a while. To keep the head from falling off before the glue sets up, use a long floral pin to hold it in place. Remove the pin after the glue has set up and dried.

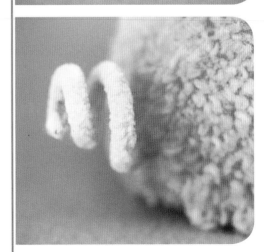

13. For the tail, cut a 4-inch (10.2 cm) length of pink pipe cleaner and twist it around a pencil to make a corkscrew. Make a part at the bottom backside of the Piglet, squeeze in a small dollop of glue, and insert the tail. Gently pinch the wool fibers around the tail to secure it. Let dry.

14. Embellish your little Piglet with a ribbon.

Squirrel

Squirrels pair curiosity and cuteness to perfection: this chap's bushy tail and inquisitive look complete his lively expression. Give him a pal or two to keep him company up in the trees by making the Bluebird or Raccoon.

1. Following steps 2–6 for Making Pompoms by Hand on pages 19–21, make a 2½-inch (6.4 cm) fat, egg-shaped pompom from gray yarn for the head. I used approximately ⅓ skein of Patons medium-weight Classic Wool, which is approximately 69 yards (63 m).

2. On the narrow end of the egg shape, locate where you want the nose to be. Make a small part into the pile of the yarn, place a small drop of glue in the part, and insert the pink seed bead. Gently pinch the fibers around the glue and the bead to secure it. Let dry.

3. Using the inverted triangle layout (see Positioning the Nose and Eyes on page 22), decide where you want the eyes to be. Make a part in the yarn, carefully squeeze in a pea-size drop of glue for each eye, and gently insert the wire end of each glass eye into the pompom. Let the glue dry.

4. Using the template on page 121, cut two ears out of the wool felt, rub the inside of each ear with a bit of pink chalk, and blend it in with your finger. Squeeze a dollop of glue onto the bottom flat part of each ear shape and pinch the lower edge together, with pink inside, to give it dimension. Repeat this for the second ear. Use clothespins or hemostats to hold the ear bases together as they dry.

5. After the ears have dried, make a small part on top of the head over each eye, squeeze a bit of glue into the pile, and insert the ears. Pinch the fibers around the ears to secure them and let dry.

6. Make another slightly larger pompom from gray yarn and trim it into a pear-shaped pompom for the body, about 4 inches (10.2 cm) tall. I used approximately ½ skein of medium-weight Patons Classic Wool, which is approximately 105 yards (96 m). The narrow top will be the Squirrel's neck, and the heavier, rounded end will be the bottom of the Squirrel sitting upright. To create the illusion of the Squirrel's haunches and tummy, trim out a V shape from the front center bottom of the belly area.

7. Glue the pipe cleaner into the top half of the pompom body. Simply make a horizontal part deep into the wool at the top, squeeze in a dime-size dollop of glue, and place the pipe cleaner snugly down into it; pinch the fibers of the wool yarn around the pipe cleaner to secure it. This will become the frame for the arms of the Squirrel, which you will needle felt. (See Creating Appendages on page 24.) Let the glue dry.

YOU WILL NEED

Basic Pompom Toolbox
(page 12)

100% wool yarn: gray

100% wool felt: gray

100% wool roving: gray

100% wool roving yarn: gray

Pink seed bead

2 black glass eyes,
10 or 12 mm

Template:
ears (page 121)

Pink chalk

6-inch (15.2 cm)
gray pipe cleaner

Needle felting supplies
(page 16)

Ribbons

Piece of a tree branch, limb,
or trunk, 3 inches (7.6 cm)
in diameter, for the base

FINISHED MEASUREMENTS
**5½ inches (14 cm) tall
(without the wooden base)**

Squirrel

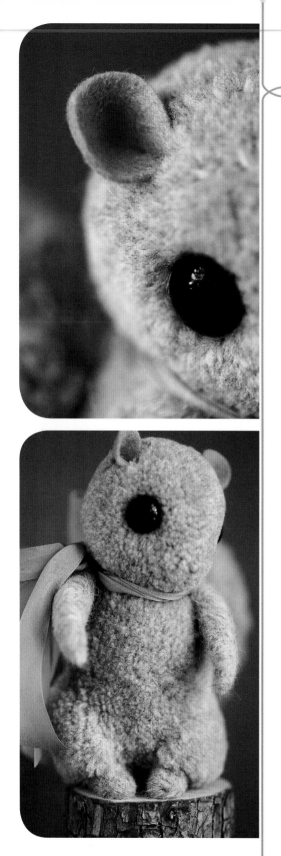

8. Glue the finished head onto the body. To create a cute, inquisitive expression, tilt the head to one side. Squeeze a nickel-size dollop of glue at the top of the body pompom and position the head as desired. You will need to let the glue set up and dry, which can take a few hours. To keep the head from falling off before the glue sets up, use a long floral pin to hold it in place. Remove the pin after the glue has set up.

9. After the glue has fully dried, bend the pipe cleaner into the desired position and trim each arm to approximately 2½ inches (6.4 cm). Bend down and crimp the sharp ends of the pipe cleaners because they will poke through the needle-felted paws.

10. Needle felt the Squirrel's feet by rolling a golf ball–size bit of wool roving into a cigarlike shape and needle felting to compact it down. Once it is a tight, dense 3-inch (7.6 cm) cigar shape, cut it evenly in half to make the two little feet.

11. At the bottom of the pear shape make two separate parts into the wool "fur" and glue and insert the feet into the body. Let it dry standing upright.

12. After the pipe cleaner and glue have set up, wrap a thick bacon-size strip of roving tightly around the pipe cleaner armatures from top to bottom. Use more roving near the upper arm and shoulder area and taper it toward the end to form a tiny paw. Needle felt the roving tightly to compact it around the pipe cleaner so it will not unravel. Bend down at the wrist to create the illusion of paws.

13. For the tail, make another pompom from wool roving yarn. I used approximately ⅓ skein of Patons bulky-weight Classic Wool Roving yarn, which is approximately 40 yards (36 m). The Squirrel's tail looks like a rounded arc with longer, fluffier roving yarn at the end, and shorter, denser roving yarn at the base. The knotted waxed twine will be located in the center of the tail's curved arc. Begin shaping the pompom by trimming the fibers on one side of the waxed twine shorter than the other side, as the shorter, denser part of the tail will be attached to the Squirrel's body. On the other side of the twine, trim the roving yarn fibers so they're slightly longer and fluffier. The longer fibers will naturally tend to droop a bit, which will create the curve of the tail. Comb the fibers with your fingers as you gradually sculpt the curved tail to approximately 6 to 7 inches (15.2 to 17.8 cm) long.

14. Make a large part in the back of the Squirrel's body and squeeze in a big dollop of glue both in the part and on the lower portion of one side of the tail; snugly insert the glued pompom tail into the part. To hold the tail in place as the glue sets up, tie a ribbon or a pipe cleaner around the tail and the body; remove it when the glue is dry. Please note that the tail often makes the Squirrel heavy in the back, so your Squirrel may tip. Gluing the Squirrel onto a simple base (like the tree section shown) will keep this from happening.

15. Tie a ribbon or two around your Squirrel's neck.

✳ NOTE: *Want to make additional embellishments for your Squirrel? Needle felt an acorn, which the Squirrel can hold in its front paws. Tiny woven baskets found in miniature shops and filled with millinery flowers, berries, or pinecones are another cute object for your Squirrel to hold.*

Squirrel

Raccoon

Don't be fooled by his endearing black mask and beguiling gaze, this Raccoon is a little woodland bandit: he might very well steal your heart.

1. Following steps 2–6 of Making Pompoms by Hand on pages 19–21, make a 2½- to 3-inch (6.4 to 7.6 cm) egg-shaped pompom from gray, cream, and black yarn for the head. Wind the yarns side by side (see Making Multicolor Pompoms on page 30) in the following order: gray, cream, black, cream. I used approximately ¼ skein of gray Patons medium-weight Classic Wool, which is approximately 53 yards (48 m); ⅛ skein, or 26 yards (24 m), of cream; ¼ skein, or 53 yards (48 m), of black; and ¼ skein, or 53 yards (48 m), of cream.

2. The gray will be at the top of the Raccoon's head. The next cream patch will be part of its face, the black will be the "mask" around the eyes, and the remaining cream patch at the edge of the pompom will be sculpted and trimmed into the Raccoon's pointed, narrow nose (see Tips on Shaping the Nose and Muzzle, page 21).

3. On the pointed snout, locate where you want the nose to be. Make a small part into the "fur," place a small drop of glue in the part, and insert the black seed bead. Pinch the fibers around the glue and the bead to secure it.

4. Using the inverted triangle layout (see Positioning the Nose and Eyes on page 22), decide where you want the eyes to be. Make a part in the yarn, carefully squeeze in a pea-size drop of glue for each eye, and gently insert the wire end of each glass eye into the pompom. Let the glue dry.

5. Using the template on page 123, cut two ears out of the gray wool felt. Make a small part on top of the head over each eye, squeeze a bit of glue into the pile, and insert the ears. Pinch the fibers around each ear to secure it and let the glue dry.

6. Following the instructions for Creating and Attaching Whiskers (page 22), thread a sewing needle with a 5-inch (12.7 cm) double strand of black upholstery thread. Tie a knot in the center, place a tiny smidge of glue on the knot, and "sew" in the whiskers. Snip off any excess so the whiskers are even on both sides.

7. Make another slightly larger pompom from gray yarn and trim it to a pear shape for the body, about 4¼ inches (10.8 cm) tall. I used approximately ½ skein of Patons medium-weight Classic Wool, which is approximately 105 yards (96 m). The narrow top

YOU WILL NEED

Basic Pompom Toolbox
(page 12)

100% wool yarn:
gray, cream, black

100% wool felt: gray

100% wool roving:
gray, black

Black seed bead

2 black glass eyes,
10 or 12 mm

Template:
ears (page 123)

Sewing needle

Black upholstery thread

6-inch (15.2 cm)
gray pipe cleaner

Needle felting supplies
(page 16)

Ribbon

FINISHED MEASUREMENTS
6½ inches (16.5 cm) tall

Raccoon

will be the Raccoon's neck and the heavier, rounded end will be the bottom of the Raccoon as it sits upright. To create the illusion of the seated Raccoon's haunches and tummy, trim out a V shape from the front center bottom of the belly area.

8. Glue the pipe cleaner into the top half of the pompom body. Simply make a horizontal part deep into the wool at the top, squeeze in a dime-size dollop of glue, and place the pipe cleaner snugly down into it. Pinch the fibers of the wool yarn around the pipe cleaner to secure it. This will become the frame for the arms of the Raccoon, which you will needle felt. (See Creating Appendages on page 24.)

9. Glue the finished head onto the body. Squeeze a nickel-size dollop of glue at the top of the body pompom and position the head as desired. To keep the head from shifting or falling off before the glue sets up, use a long floral pin to hold it in place. Remove the pin after the glue has set up and dried.

10. After the glue has fully dried, bend the pipe cleaners into the desired position and trim each arm to approximately 2½ inches (6.4 cm). Bend down and tightly crimp the sharp cut ends of the pipe cleaners because they will poke through the needle-felted paws.

11. Take a thick bacon-size strip of gray roving and wrap it tightly around the pipe cleaner arms. Use more roving near the upper arm and shoulder area and taper off at the end to form a tiny paw. Needle felt the roving tightly to make it compact around the pipe cleaner so it will not unravel (see Needle Felting Appendages on page 24). Needle felt black roving to the front paws as well, so the Raccoon has little black socks. Shave off excess "fuzzies" with scissors for a neater appearance, if desired.

12. Make the Raccoon's feet by rolling a golf ball–size bit of black roving into a cigarlike shape and start needle felting to compact it down. Once it is a tight, dense 3-inch (7.6 cm) cigar shape, cut it evenly in half to make the two feet.

13. At the bottom of the pear shape make two separate slits into the wool "fur" and glue the hind feet into the body, adjusting them as necessary so the Raccoon sits upright. Let dry.

14. For the tail, wind the gray and black yarns side by side (see Making Multicolor Pompoms on page 30) in the following order: gray, black, gray, black. I used approximately ⅓ skein of gray Patons medium-weight Classic Wool, which is approximately 69 yards (63 m); ⅛ skein, or 26 yards (24 m) of black; ⅛ skein, or 26 yards (24 m) of gray; and ⅛ skein, or 26 yards (24 m) of black. Instead of trimming the pompom into a ball shape, however, trim it into a straighter torpedo shape approximately 6 inches (15.2 cm) in length with the black end yarn at the tip of the Raccoon's tail.

15. For added structural security when attaching the tail, snip a piece of pipe cleaner approximately 1 to 2 inches (2.5 to 5.1 cm) and glue it into the end of the tail that will be attached to the body. Let dry. Make a part at the bottom backside, squeeze a dollop of glue into the part, and gently but snugly insert the end of the tail with the attached pipe cleaner. Gently pinch the wool fibers to secure the tail. To hold the tail in place on the body as the glue sets up, tie a ribbon or a pipe cleaner around the tail and the body, then remove it when the glue is dry.

16. Embellish your Raccoon with a ribbon.

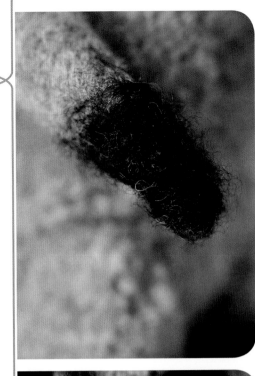

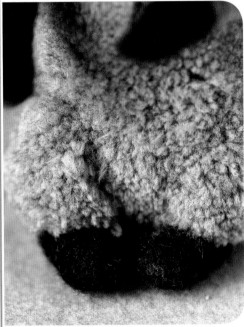

Hedgehog

You won't have to avoid prickly spikes on this little guy—his soft, fluffy backside is made with wool roving yarn, and his sweet expression is just meant for company. Perhaps he's waiting for his woodland friends, Raccoon and Fox, to come for tea.

1. Following steps 2–6 of Making Pompoms by Hand on pages 19–21, make a 3-inch (7.6 cm) pompom from both brown roving yarn and cream wool yarn for the head. Wind the yarns side by side (see Making Multicolor Pompoms on page 30); I used approximately ¼ skein of Patons bulky-weight Classic Wool Roving yarn, which is approximately 30 yards (27 m), in brown, and approximately ¼ skein of Patons Classic Wool, which is approximately 53 yards (48 m), in cream.

2. The cream yarn will become the Hedgehog's face; move all the cream yarn to one side of the pompom. Sculpt and trim the cream yarn into a more pointed and narrower shape for the Hedgehog's snout and nose (see Tips on Shaping the Nose and Muzzle, page 21). Continue to carefully trim and shave down the cream yarn only, cutting it approximately ¼ inch (6 mm) lower than the fluffier brown roving yarn. The longer brown roving yarn forms the Hedgehog's spiky hair on its head.

3. On the cream yarn at the narrow end of the egg shape, locate where you want the nose to be. Make a small part into the "fur" of the yarn, place a small drop of glue, and insert the black seed bead. Pinch the fibers around the glue and the bead to secure it. Let the glue dry.

4. Using the inverted triangle layout (see Positioning the Nose and Eyes on page 22), decide where you want the eyes to be. Make a part in the yarn, carefully squeeze in a pea-size drop of glue for each eye, and gently insert the wire end of each glass eye into the pompom. Let the glue dry.

5. Using the template on page 121, cut two ears out of the cream wool felt. Rub the inside of each ear with pink chalk and blend it in with your finger. Make a small part between the brown roving yarn and the cream face yarn over each eye, squeeze a bit of glue into the parts, and insert the ears. Pinch the fibers around the ears to secure them and let them dry.

6. Make another slightly larger pompom by mixing brown roving yarn and cream wool yarn and trim it into a slightly pear-shaped pompom for the body, about 3¾ inches (9.5 cm) tall. I used approximately ⅓ skein of brown Patons bulky-weight Classic Wool Roving yarn, which is approximately 40 yards (36 m), and ⅓ skein

YOU WILL NEED

Basic Pompom Toolbox
(page 12)

100% wool yarn:
cream

100% wool felt:
cream

100% wool roving yarn:
brown

100% wool roving:
brown

Black seed bead

2 black glass eyes,
10 or 12 mm

Template:
ears (page 121)

Pink chalk

6-inch (15.2 cm) pipe cleaner

Needle felting supplies
(page 16)

Ribbon

FINISHED MEASUREMENTS
6 ½ inches (16.5 cm) tall

Hedgehog

of cream Patons medium-weight Classic Wool, which is approximately 69 yards (63 m). The cream yarn will be the Hedgehog's tummy. Using the heavier, fuller end of the pompom as the bottom, start shaping and trimming the pompom into a rounded shape. To create the definition of the Hedgehog's tummy and haunches, carefully trim cream yarn on the center bottom of the belly area (see Shaping Pompoms page 29). Allow the brown roving yarn to remain a bit longer like the spiky hair around the face.

7. Glue the pipe cleaner into the top half of the pompom body. Simply make a horizontal part deep into the wool at the top, squeeze a dime-size dollop of glue, and place the pipe cleaner snugly down into it; pinch the fibers of the wool yarn to secure it. This will become the frame for the arms of the Hedgehog, which you will needle felt. (See Creating Appendages on page 24.)

8. Glue the finished head onto the body. To create a cute, inquisitive expression, tilt the head to one side. Squeeze a nickel-size dollop of glue at the top of the body pompom and position the head as desired. To keep the head from shifting or falling off before the glue sets, use a long floral pin to hold it in place until dry. Remove the pin after the glue has set up and dried.

9. After the glue has fully dried, bend the pipe cleaners into the desired position and trim each arm to approximately 2½ inches (6.4 cm). Bend down and tightly crimp the sharp ends of the pipe cleaners because they will poke through the needle-felted ends of the paws.

10. Needle felt the Hedgehog's feet by rolling a golf ball–size bit of brown roving into a cigarlike shape and start needle felting to compact it down (see Attaching Feet and Small Appendages on page 26). Once it is a tight, compact 3-inch (7.6 cm) cigar shape, cut it evenly in half to make the two feet.

11. At the bottom of the body pompom make two separate slits into the wool "fur" and glue the hind feet into the body. Let it dry sitting upright.

12. After the pipe cleaner and glue have set up, take a thick, bacon-size strip of roving and wrap it tightly around the pipe cleaner arms. Use more roving near the upper top of the arm and shoulder area and taper it off at the end to form a tiny paw. Needle felt the roving tightly to make it compact around the pipe cleaner so it will not unravel (see Needle Felting Appendages on page 24).

13. Tie a ribbon around your Hedgehog's neck.

Fox

Foxes are often referred to as the thieves of the animal kingdom, and this little fox is sure to steal your heart.

1. Following steps 2–5 of Making Pompoms by Hand on pages 19–21, make a round ball-shaped pompom from both orange and white yarns for the head. Wind the yarns side by side (see Making Multicolor Pompoms on page 30); I used approximately ⅓ skein of orange Patons medium-weight Classic Wool, which is approximately 69 yards (63 m), and ¼ skein, which is approximately 53 yards (48 m), of white.

2. The Fox's face is orange with a white chin. Assess your pompom and determine how you will begin trimming and sculpting the rough, uneven ball into a smooth, sculpted egg shape, 3 inches (7.6 cm) in diameter, with the top of the head in orange and the bottom in white. The Fox's nose should fall roughly where the orange and white yarns meet. With this in mind, trim the narrow end of the egg shape into the nose, sculpting it to be more tapered and pointy. (See Tips on Shaping the Nose and Muzzle, page 21.)

3. Locate where you want the nose to be between the orange and white yarn and make a small part into the "fur." Place a small drop of glue and insert a black seed bead for the nose. Pinch the fibers around the glue and bead to secure it. Let dry.

4. Using the inverted triangle layout (see Positioning the Nose and Eyes on page 22), decide where you want the eyes to be. Make a part in the yarn, carefully squeeze in a pea-size drop of glue for each eye, and gently insert the wire end of each glass eye into the pompom. Let the glue dry.

5. Using the template on page 123, cut two triangular ears from the orange wool felt. Rub some black chalk around the outer edge of the ears, if desired.

6. Make a small part on top of the head over each eye and squeeze a bit of glue into the part of the wool fibers; insert the ears. Pinch the fibers around the base of the ears to secure them, and let dry.

7. Following the instructions for Creating and Attaching Whiskers on page 22, thread a sewing needle with a 5-inch (12.7 cm) double strand of black upholstery thread. Tie a knot in the middle, place a tiny smidge of glue on the knot, and "sew" in the short whiskers. The knot should be positioned approximately in the center front of the head. Snip off any excess so the whiskers are even on both sides.

YOU WILL NEED

Basic Pompom Toolbox
(page 12)

100% wool yarn: orange, white or cream, black

100% wool felt: orange

100% wool roving: orange, black (optional)

Black seed bead

2 black glass eyes, 10 or 12 mm

Template: ears (page 123)

Black chalk (optional)

Sewing needle

Black upholstery thread

8-inch (20.3 cm) orange pipe cleaner

2-inch (5.1 cm) orange pipe cleaner

Needle felting supplies (see page 16)

FINISHED MEASUREMENTS
6 inches (15.2 cm) tall

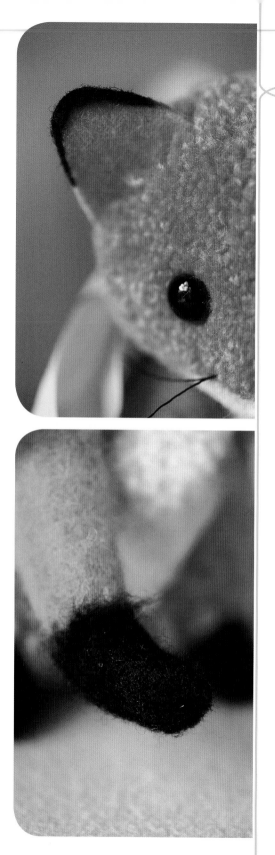

8. Make another slightly larger pompom and trim it into a 4¼-inch (10.7 cm) pear-shaped pompom for the body, again mixing orange and white yarns side by side. I used approximately ½ skein of orange Patons medium-weight Classic Wool, which is approximately 105 yards (96 m), and approximately ⅓ skein, or 69 yards (63 m), of white. The white yarn will become the Fox's tummy. The narrower top of the pompom will be the Fox's neck, and the heavier, rounded end will become the bottom of the Fox as it sits upright. To create the illusion of the Fox's haunches and tummy, carefully trim the white yarn into a V shape on the center bottom of the white belly area.

9. Glue the 8-inch (20.3 cm) pipe cleaner into the top half of the pompom body. Make a part in the top of the narrow end of the pompom body. Squeeze in a dime-size dollop of glue. Place the pipe cleaner snugly down into the part, and pinch the fibers of the wool yarn to secure it. This will become the frame for the arms of the Fox, which you will needle felt. (See Creating Appendages on page 24.)

10. Glue the finished head onto the body. Squeeze in a nickel-size dollop of glue at the top of the body pompom and position the head as desired. You will need to let the glue set up and dry, which can take a while. To keep the head from falling off before the glue sets up, use a long floral pin to hold it in place. Remove the pin after the glue has set up and dried.

11. After the glue has fully dried, bend the pipe cleaner into the desired position and trim each arm to approximately 3 inches (7.6 cm). Bend down and tightly crimp the sharp cut ends of the pipe cleaners because they can poke through and show at the ends of the needle-felted paws.

12. Needle felt the Fox's hind feet by rolling a golf ball–size bit of orange roving into a cigarlike shape and start needle felting to compact it (see Attaching Feet and Small Appendages on page 26). Once it is a tight, dense 3-inch (7.6 cm) cigar shape, cut it evenly in half to make the two back paws. If you wish, needle felt black roving onto the end of these paws.

13. At the bottom of the pear-shaped body, make two separate long slits into the wool "fur" and glue the feet into the body. Let it dry sitting upright.

14. After the glue has set up, take a thick bacon-size strip of roving and wrap it tightly, top to bottom, around the pipe cleaner arms. Use more roving near the upper arm and shoulder area and taper off at the end to form a paw. Needle felt the roving tightly to make it compact around the pipe cleaner so it will not unravel (see Needle Felting Appendages on page 24). Needle felt black roving to the front paws as well, so the Fox has little black socks. Shave off excess "fuzzies" with scissors for a neater appearance, if desired.

15. For the tail, make an additional 6-inch (15.2 cm) pompom, again winding the orange and white yarn side by side. I used approximately 1/3 skein of orange Patons medium-weight Classic Wool, which is approximately 69 yards (63 m), and 1/4 skein, which is approximately 53 yards (48 m), of white. Instead of trimming the pompom into a ball shape, however, trim it into a straighter torpedo shape approximately 6 inches (15.2 cm) in length with the white yarn at the tip of the Fox's tail.

16. For added structural security when attaching the tail, snip a piece of pipe cleaner approximately 1 to 2 inches (2.5 to 5.1 cm) and glue it into the end of the tail that will be attached to the body. Let dry. Make a part at the bottom backside, squeeze a dollop of glue into the part, and gently but snugly insert the end of the tail with the attached pipe cleaner. Gently pinch the wool fibers to secure the tail. You can use a piece of ribbon or an extra pipe cleaner to temporarily tie the tail to the Fox's body pompom as it dries in place.

✳ **NOTE:** *If you cannot find matching orange wool felt and orange yarn, you can dye cream-colored yarn, roving, and wool felt using orange dye found in many craft and grocery stores. Simply follow the directions on the package to make custom colors.*

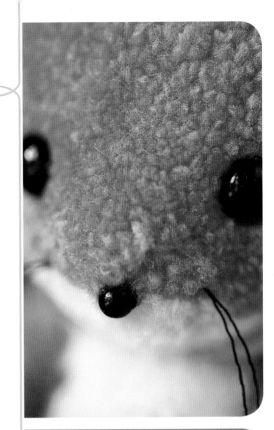

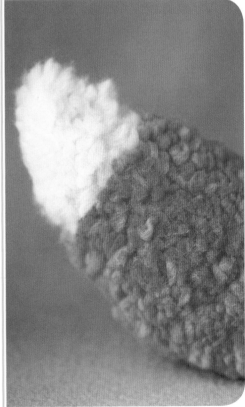

Pony

For all of us who wished we had a pony in our childhood, here's our chance!
Move over, Black Beauty: this pompom cutie is galloping onto the scene.

1. Following steps 2–6 of Making Pompoms by Hand on pages 19–21, make a 3-inch (7.6 cm) smooth, fat, egg-shaped pompom from white or cream yarn for the head. I used approximately ⅓ skein of Patons medium-weight Classic Wool, which is approximately 69 yards (63 m).

2. On the narrow end of the shaped pompom, locate where you want the nose to be. Make two small marks with pink chalk for the nostrils and blend them in with your finger.

3. Using the inverted triangle pattern (see Positioning the Nose and Eyes, page 22), decide where you want the eyes to be; ponies' eyes are typically spaced far apart, one on each side of the head. Make a part in the yarn, carefully squeeze in a pea-size drop of glue for each eye, and gently insert the wire end of each glass eye into the pompom. Let the glue dry.

4. Using the template on page 123, cut two ears out of the wool felt. Rub pink chalk inside each ear and blend it in with your finger. To create dimension, place a bit of glue along the straight bottom of each ear and pinch the edges together, with the pink inside. Use clothespins or hemostats to hold the ear bases in place while they dry.

5. After the ears have dried, make a tiny part in the wool on top of the head over each eye and squeeze a bit of glue into the wool fibers; insert the ears. Pinch the fibers around the base of the ears to secure them and let dry.

6. Make another slightly larger pompom from white yarn and trim it into a fat bun-shaped pompom for the body measuring approximately 4 inches (10.2) in length and diameter. I used approximately ½ skein of Patons medium-weight Classic Wool, which is approximately 105 yards (96 m).

7. To create the Pony's legs, use your wire cutters to cut four equal pieces from the wooden dowel to create legs approximately 3 inches (7.6 cm) long.

8. Wrap each leg thickly in wool roving and needle felt around the dowel (see Needle Felting Appendages on page 24). Needle felt the roving tightly; the upper end should be slightly thicker than the bottom of the leg and the back legs should be a bit thicker than

YOU WILL NEED

Basic Pompom Toolbox
(page 12)

100% wool yarn:
white or cream

100% wool felt:
white or cream

100% wool roving:
white or cream

100% wool roving yarn:
white or cream

Pink chalk

2 black glass eyes,
10 or 12 mm

Template:
ears (page 123)

Wire cutters

12-inch (30.5 cm) wooden
dowel, 5 mm in diameter

Needle felting supplies
(page 16)

6-inch (15.2 cm)
white pipe cleaner

Ribbon

Millinery flowers

FINISHED MEASUREMENTS
**5¼ inches (13.3 cm) tall
at the top of the back;
7½ inches (19 cm) tall
at the top of the head**

Pony

✳ **NOTE:** *You can turn this Pony into a magical Unicorn by needle felting a thin, white cone-shaped horn and gluing it into the forehead.*

the front legs. Be sure to needle felt over the bottom of the dowels so they are not exposed. Shave off any excess "fuzzies" with scissors for a neater appearance, if desired.

9. Make four deep parts on the bottom of the Pony's body where you want to position the legs. Add glue in each part and insert the legs, firmly pinching the wool fibers around the legs to secure them. Adjust the legs as necessary so the Pony can stand. Let it dry standing upright.

10. To make the Pony's neck, fold the pipe cleaner in half. Cut the two ends so it is approximately 2 1/2 inches (6.4 cm) in length. Take a thick piece of wool roving and wrap it around the pipe cleaner to make a fat cylindrical shape about 1 3/4 inches (4.4 cm) in diameter at the base and 1 1/4 inches (3.2 cm) in diameter at the top. Needle felt and compact the fibers down tightly. Trim any excess "fuzzies," if desired.

11. With the pipe cleaners sticking out of each end of the neck, the thicker part of the neck will be glued to the body. Squeeze a nickel-size dollop of glue into the body pompom and insert the neck. Pinch the fibers around the neck to secure it. Let dry.

12. Glue the finished head onto the top of the neck. You will need to let the glue set up and dry, which can take a while. To keep the head from shifting or falling off before the glue sets up, lay the Pony on its side and use a long floral pin to hold the head in place until dry. Remove the pin after the glue has set up and dried.

13. For the tail, cut approximately twelve 4-inch (10.2 cm) pieces of wool roving yarn. Tie the ends together. Make a part at the bottom backside, squeeze in a small dollop of glue, and gently insert the knotted end of the tail. Gently pinch the wool fibers around the tail to secure it. Let dry.

14. To create the mane, tie wool roving yarn into approximately ten bundles of 2-inch long (5.1 cm) strands. Using the sharp, pointed ends of the scissors, puncture holes along the top of the neck and head and squeeze in a bit of glue. Stuff the knotted ends of the bundles into the holes and pinch the fibers around the yarn bundles to secure them. Let dry. Trim the mane so it is shorter by the ears and eyes and longer on the neck.

15. Embellish your Pony with a ribbon and millinery flowers, as desired.

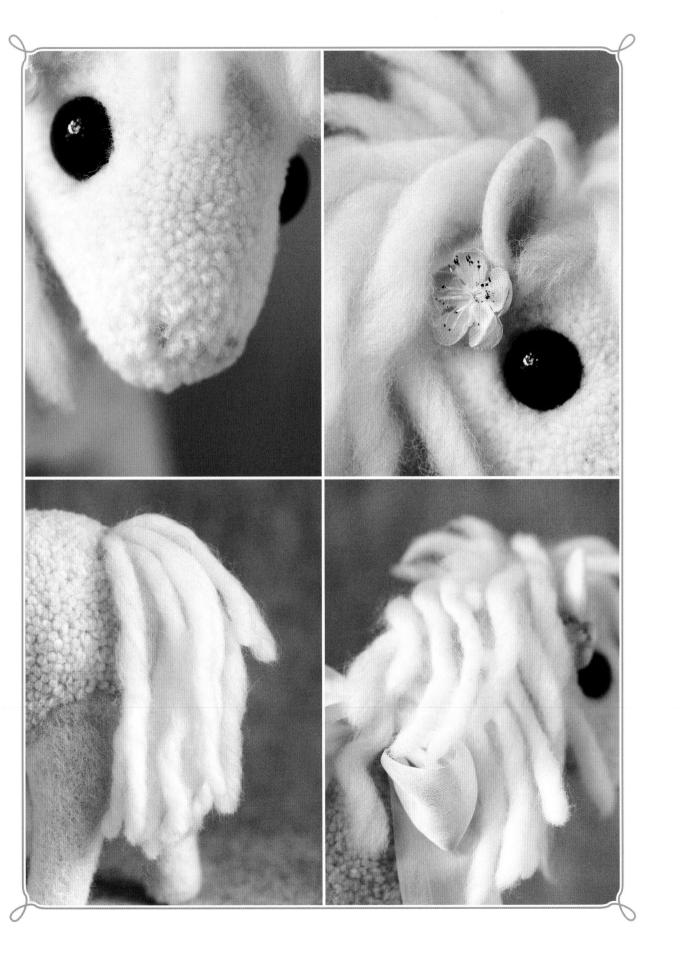

Snowy Owl

This fine-feathered friend is made with both yarn and roving yarn, which gives his tail feathers their longer, fluffier look. Try using larger glass eyes to give him an owlish gaze.

1. Following steps 2–6 of Making Pompoms by Hand on pages 19–21, make a 3-inch (7.6 cm) oval-shaped pompom from both bulky-weight white roving yarn and medium-weight cream yarn for the head. Wind the yarns side by side (see Making Multicolor Pompoms on page 30); I used approximately ⅓ skein of Patons Classic Wool Roving, which is approximately 40 yards (36 m), and approximately ⅛ skein of Patons Classic Wool, which is approximately 26 yards (24 m). The roving yarn is chunkier and thicker, which better lends itself to create the illusion of feathers; the other yarn will be sculpted to become the smooth part of the Owl's face.

2. Although both yarns are the same color, you will be able to see the difference between the textures of the roving yarn and the regular wool yarn. Push, pull, and gently manipulate the regular yarn to one side of the pompom, which will become the front of the Owl's head and face. Begin shaping and trimming the regular wool yarn into a heart shape, cutting it ¼ inch (6 mm) lower than the fluffier roving yarn. This area defines the Owl's face.

3. Using the inverted triangle layout (see Positioning the Nose and Eyes on page 22), decide where you want the eyes to be. Make a part in the yarn, carefully squeeze in a pea-size drop of glue for each eye, and gently insert the wire end of each glass eye into the pompom. Let the glue dry.

4. Using the template on page 121, cut out the beak shape from beige wool felt.

5. Place the beak in the center of the face area. Make a small part into the pile of the yarn and place a small drop of glue. Attach the beak. Gently pinch the fibers around the glue and the felt beak to secure it. Let the glue dry.

6. Make another slightly larger pompom from the roving yarn and trim it into an oblong bun-shaped pompom for the body, about 4½ inches (11.4 cm) tall and about 6 inches (15.2 cm) from the front of the chest to the tip of the tail feathers. I used approximately ½ skein of Patons bulky-weight Classic Wool Roving yarn, which is approximately 60 yards (55 m). Leave the roving yarn longer on one end to cut and shape the fluffy tail feathers.

YOU WILL NEED

Basic Pompom Toolbox
(page 12)

100% wool yarn:
cream

100% wool felt:
beige

100% wool roving yarn:
cream

2 black glass eyes,
14 mm

Template:
beak (page 121)

32 inches (81.3 cm) of
18-gauge floral wire

Embroidery floss or
perle cotton:
yellow or orange

Ribbon

FINISHED MEASUREMENTS
7 ¾ inches (19.7 cm) tall

Snowy Owl

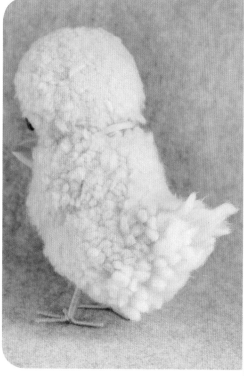

7. Place the oval head on the body horizontally. To create a cute, inquisitive expression, tilt the head to one side. Squeeze a nickel-size dollop of glue at the top of the body pompom and position the head as desired. You will need to let the glue set up and dry, which can take a few hours. To keep the head from falling off before the glue sets up, use a long floral pin to hold it in place. Remove the pin after the glue has set up and dried.

8. Using wire cutters, cut eight 4-inch (10.2 cm) pieces of floral wire.

9. To create each foot, hold four pieces of wire together and lightly coat the bundle with glue. Working from top to bottom, wind the embroidery floss or perle cotton tightly and uniformly around the bundle of four wires. Stop approximately 1½ inches (3.8 cm) from the bottom. Bend each of the four wires out at 90° angles to make individual toes. Three will face forward; one will face backward to provide the support needed for the bird to stand. Continue wrapping each "toe" wire individually with embroidery floss to cover the floral wire. Repeat with the remaining four pieces of floral wire to create the other leg. Use wire cutters to snip off any excess wire length. Tuck any ends of embroidery floss underneath and let the glue dry.

10. At the bottom of the Owl's body, make two separate parts into the wool plush for the legs and squeeze a dollop of glue into each. Insert the wire legs snugly into the body. Pinch the wool fibers around the wrapped wires to secure them. Set the Snowy Owl upright and make any adjustments necessary so that it can stand. Let it dry in this position.

11. Tie a ribbon around your Snowy Owl's neck.

Halloween Imp

A roguish little imp can be a playful project for Halloween or perhaps a mischievous companion to a Valentine's Day cherub.

YOU WILL NEED

Basic Pompom Toolbox
(page 12)

100% wool yarn:
bright red

100% wool felt:
bright red, black

100% wool roving:
bright red

Pink seed bead

2 black glass eyes,
10 or 12 mm

Templates: ears, horns, tail,
pitchfork (page 122)

Two 6-inch (15.2 cm)
red pipe cleaners

Needle felting supplies
(page 16)

4-inch (10.2 cm) length
of wooden dowel,
2 mm in diameter

Wire cutters

Black craft paint

Paintbrush

Black ribbon (optional)

FINISHED MEASUREMENTS

**Imp: 5 ¾ inches
(14.6 cm) tall
Pitchfork: 6 inches
(15.2 cm) tall**

1. Following steps 2–6 of Making Pompoms by Hand on pages 19–21, make a 2½- to 3-inch (6.4 to 7.6 cm) smooth, round, ball-shaped pompom from bright red yarn for the head. I used approximately ⅓ skein of Patons medium-weight Classic Wool, which is approximately 69 yards (63 m).

2. Locate the center of the pompom where you want the nose to be and make a small part into the yarn. Squeeze in a small drop of glue and insert a pink seed bead. Pinch the fibers around the glue and bead to secure it. Let dry.

3. Using the inverted triangle layout (see Positioning the Nose and Eyes on page 22), decide where you want the eyes to be. Make a part in the yarn, carefully squeeze in a pea-size drop of glue for each eye, and gently insert the wire end of each glass eye into the pompom. Let the glue dry.

4. Using the templates on page 122, cut two ears and two horns out of the red wool felt.

5. Make a small part on top of the head over each eye and squeeze a bit of glue into each part; insert the horns. Pinch the fibers around each horn to secure it, and let dry.

6. On each side of the head make a small part and squeeze a drop or two of glue into the part; insert the ears. Pinch the fibers around each ear to secure it and let dry.

7. Make another slightly larger pompom from red yarn and trim it into a pear shape for the body, about 4 inches (10.2 cm) tall. I used approximately ½ skein of Patons medium-weight Classic Wool, which is approximately 105 yards (96 m). The narrow top will be the Imp's neck and the heavier, rounded end will be the bottom of the Imp as it sits upright. To create the illusion of the Imp's haunches and tummy, trim out a V shape from the front center bottom of the belly area.

8. Glue a pipe cleaner into the top half of the pompom body. Simply make a horizontal part deep into the wool at the top, squeeze in a dime-size dollop of glue, and place the pipe cleaner snugly down into the part; pinch the wool fibers around the pipe cleaner to secure it. This will become the frame for the arms of the Imp, which you will needle felt. (See Creating Appendages on page 24.)

Halloween Imp

9. Glue the finished head onto the body. Squeeze a nickel-size dollop of glue at the top of the body pompom and position the head as desired. To keep the head from falling off before the glue sets up, use a long floral pin to hold it in place until dry. Remove the pin after the glue has set up and dried.

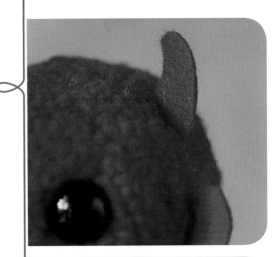

10. After the glue has fully dried, bend the pipe cleaner into the desired arm position and trim each arm to approximately 2½ inches (6.4 cm). Bend down and tightly crimp the sharp cut ends of the pipe cleaners because they will poke through the needle-felted ends.

11. Needle felt the Imp's feet by rolling a golf ball–size bit of red roving into a cigarlike shape and start needle felting to compact it down (see Attaching Feet and Small Appendages on page 26). Once it is a tight, dense 3-inch (7.6 cm) cigar shape, cut it evenly in half to make the two feet.

12. At the bottom of the pear shape make two separate slits into the wool "fur" and glue the hind feet into the body. Let it dry standing upright.

13. After the pipe cleaner and glue have set up, take a thick bacon-size strip of the red roving and wrap it tightly, top to bottom, around the pipe cleaner arms. Use more roving near the upper arm and shoulder area and taper off at the end to form a tiny hand. Needle felt the roving tightly to make it compact around the pipe cleaner so it will not unravel (see Needle Felting Appendages on page 24).

14. For the tail, cut a 5-inch (12.7 cm) piece of red pipe cleaner, and using the template on page 122, cut out a triangle from red felt and glue it securely to the end of the pipe cleaner. On the bottom backside of the devil make a part in the wool fiber, add some glue, and insert the tail. Pinch the wool fibers around to secure it. Let dry.

15. To create a tiny pitchfork for your little Imp to hold, cut off a 4-inch (10.2 cm) piece of the wooden dowel with wire cutters and paint it black. Let dry. Using the template on page 122, cut out the pitchfork's trident pattern from black felt and glue it onto the end of the dowel.

16. Place the pitchfork in the little Imp's hand and needle felt or glue it into place.

✳ **NOTE:** *You can also tie a black ribbon around the Imp's neck, if desired.*

Halloween Imp

Halloween Bat

Too cute to be scary, this little bat is sure to make someone smile on Halloween.

1. Following steps 2–6 of Making Pompoms by Hand on pages 19–21, make a 2½-inch (6.4 cm) round ball-shaped pompom from purple yarn for the head. I used approximately ⅓ skein of Patons medium-weight Classic Wool, which is approximately 69 yards (63 m).

2. Locate the center of the pompom where you want the nose to be and make a small part into the yarn, place a small drop of glue, and insert the pink seed bead. Pinch the fibers around the glue and bead to secure it. Let dry.

3. Using the inverted triangle layout (see Positioning the Nose and Eyes on page 22), decide where you want the eyes to be. Make a part in the yarn, carefully squeeze in a pea-size drop of glue for each eye, and gently insert the wire end of each glass eye into the pompom. Let the glue dry.

4. Using the template on page 121, cut two ears from the wool felt. Rub a little pink chalk inside each ear and blend it in with your finger. Place glue on the flat end of one ear and pinch the edge together, with the pink chalk inside, to create dimension. Repeat this for the second ear. Use clothespins or hemostats to hold the ear bases together until they are dry.

YOU WILL NEED

Basic Pompom Toolbox
(page 12)

100% wool yarn:
purple

100% wool felt:
purple

100% wool roving:
purple

Pink seed bead

2 black glass eyes,
10 or 12 mm

Templates:
ears, wings (page 121)

Pink chalk

Needle felting supplies
(page 16)

Black ribbon

FINISHED MEASUREMENTS
5½ inches (14 cm) tall

Halloween Bat

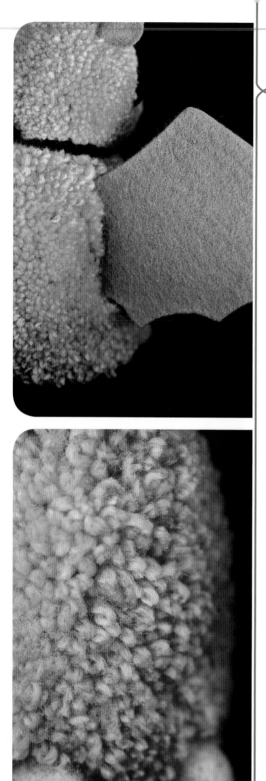

5. Make a small part on top of the head over each eye and squeeze in a bit of glue. Insert the ears and pinch the wool fibers around the ears to secure them. Let dry.

6. Make another slightly larger pompom from the purple yarn and trim it into a pear shape for the body, about 4 inches (10.2 cm) tall. I used approximately ½ skein of Patons medium-weight Classic Wool, which is approximately 105 yards (96 m). The narrower top will be the Bat's neck, and the heavier, rounded end will be the bottom of the Bat as it sits upright.

7. Using the template on page 121, cut two wings from the purple wool felt. Make a deep vertical part on the right side of the Bat's body. Squeeze a line of glue into the part and place the edge of a felt wing snugly into the part, pinching the fibers of the wool yarn to secure it. Repeat this process for the left wing and let the glue dry completely.

8. Glue the finished head onto the body. Squeeze a nickel-size dollop of glue at the top of the body pompom and position the head as desired. To keep the head from falling off before the glue sets up, use a long floral pin to hold it in place. Remove the pin after the glue has set up and dried.

9. Needle felt the Bat's feet by rolling a golf ball–size bit of roving into a cigarlike shape and start needle felting to compact it down (see Attaching Feet and Small Appendages on page 26). Once it is a tight, dense 3-inch (7.6 cm) cigar shape, cut it evenly in half to make the two feet.

10. At the bottom of the body make two separate slits into the wool "fur" and glue the hind feet into the body. Let it dry standing upright.

11. Tie a black ribbon around the Bat's neck, with the bow in back.

Halloween Bat

Halloween Black Cat

Black cats on Halloween are traditionally meant to be spooky,
but this little guy is nothing but sweet.

Basic Pompom Toolbox
(page 12)

100% wool yarn:
black

100% wool felt:
black

100% wool roving:
black

Pink seed bead

2 black glass eyes,
10 or 12 mm

Template:
ears (page 123)

Sewing needle

White upholstery thread

2 black pipe cleaners,
6 inches (15.2 cm) and
8 inches (20.3 cm) long

Needle felting supplies
(page 16)

Orange ribbon

Small drawstring jewelry or
muslin sachet bag (optional)

3-inch (7.6 cm) wooden disk,
decorated with paint, glitter,
and rickrack (optional)

FINISHED MEASUREMENTS
**5 ³/₄ inches (14.6 cm) tall,
without base**

1. Following steps 2–6 of Making Pompoms by Hand on pages 19–21, make a 2¹/₂-inch (6.4 cm) smooth, fat, egg-shaped pompom from black yarn for the head. I used approximately ¹/₃ skein of Patons medium-weight Classic Wool, which is approximately 69 yards (63 m).

2. On the narrow end of the egg shape, locate where you want the nose to be. Make a small part into the "fur," squeeze in a small drop of glue, and insert the pink seed bead. Pinch the fibers around the glue and the bead to secure it. Let the glue dry.

3. Using the inverted triangle layout (see Positioning the Nose and Eyes on page 22), decide where you want the eyes to be. Make a part in the yarn, carefully squeeze in a pea-size drop of glue for each eye, and gently insert the wire end of each glass eye into the pompom. Let the glue dry.

4. Using the template on page 123, cut two ears out of the wool felt.

5. Make a small part on the top of the head over each eye and squeeze a bit of glue into each part. Insert the ears and pinch the fibers around the base of the ears to secure them. Let dry.

6. Following the instructions for Creating and Attaching Whiskers (page 22), thread a sewing needle with a 5-inch (12.7 cm) double strand of upholstery thread. Tie a knot in the middle of the double strand, place a tiny smidge of glue on the knot, and "sew" in the whiskers. The knot should be approximately in the center front of the head. Snip off any excess so the whiskers are even on both sides.

7. Make another slightly larger pompom from the black yarn and trim it into a pear shape for the body, about 3³/₄ inches (9.5 cm) tall. I used approximately ¹/₂ skein of Patons medium-weight Classic Wool, which is approximately 105 yards (96 m). The narrow top will be the Cat's neck and the heavier, rounded end will become the bottom of the Cat as it sits upright. To create the illusion of the Cat's haunches and tummy, carefully trim out a V shape from the center bottom of the pear shape on the pompom's front side.

8. Glue the 6-inch (15.2 cm) pipe cleaner into the top half of the pompom body. Simply make a horizontal part deep into the wool at the top, squeeze in a dime-size dollop of glue, and place the pipe cleaner snugly down into it. Pinch the fibers of the wool yarn around it to secure the pipe cleaner. This will become the frame for the arms of the Cat, which you will needle felt. (See Creating Appendages on page 24.)

9. Glue the finished head onto the body. To create a cute, inquisitive expression, tilt the head to one side. Squeeze a nickel-size dollop of glue at the top of the body pompom and position the head as desired. You will need to let the glue set up and dry, which can take a while. To keep the head from falling off before the glue sets up, use a long floral pin to hold it in place. Remove the pin after the glue has set up and dried.

10. After the pipe cleaner and glue have fully dried, bend the pipe cleaners into the desired position and trim each arm to approximately 3 inches (7.6 cm). Bend down and tightly crimp the sharp cut ends of the pipe cleaners because they can poke through and show out the end of the needle-felted paws.

11. Needle felt the Cat's hind feet by rolling a golf ball–size bit of roving into a cigarlike shape and start needle felting to compact it down (see Attaching Feet and Small Appendages on page 26). Once it is a tight, dense 3-inch (7.6 cm) cigar shape, cut it evenly in half to make the two back paws.

12. At the bottom of the pear shape make two separate long slits into the wool "fur" and glue the feet into the body. Let it dry sitting upright.

13. After the pipe cleaner and glue have set up, take a thick bacon-size strip of roving and wrap it tightly, top to bottom, around the pipe cleaner arms. Use more roving near the upper arm and shoulder area and taper off at the end to form a tiny paw. Needle felt the roving tightly to make it compact around the pipe cleaner so it will not unravel (see Needle Felting Appendages on page 24). Trim off excess "fuzzies" with scissors for a neater appearance, if desired.

14. For the tail, wrap roving tightly around the 8-inch (20.3 cm) pipe cleaner. Place a bit more roving toward one end, which will attach to the body, and let it taper off at the other end, which becomes the tip of the tail. Needle felt the entire tail evenly so the roving does not unravel. When finished, make a part at the bottom backside of the body pompom, squeeze in a small dollop of glue, and gently insert the tail. Gently pinch the wool fibers around the tail to secure it. Let dry. Curl the tail to your preference.

15. To embellish your Cat for Halloween, tie an orange ribbon around its neck and use a little drawstring jewelry or muslin sachet bag as a trick-or-treat sack for the Cat to hold in its front paws. As another option, paint and embellish a smooth wooden disk to create a base for your pompom Cat.

✳ **NOTE:** *Additional embellishments for the Halloween Black Cat include a tiny papier-mâché pumpkin to hold in its paws or a pointed hat formed from a 3-inch (7.6 cm) circle of black felt that you cut in half; you can leave it like a clown's hat and attach little pompoms or fashion it into a witch's hat by adding a big circular brim. Purple and black ribbons are also nice to use for Halloween.*

Thanksgiving Turkey

Giving thanks never looked so cute! This dandy-looking Turkey makes a wonderful take-home gift for guests at Thanksgiving. Use multiple Toms to decorate your table; they can even serve as place-card holders for a holiday dinner.

Basic Pompom Toolbox
(page 12)

100% wool yarn:
red, brown

100% wool felt:
orange, brown, beige, cream,
dark brown

Templates:
beak (page 121), tail (page 122),
top hat (page 124)

2 black glass eyes,
10 or 12 mm

Wire cutters

32 inches (81.3 cm)
of 18-gauge floral wire

Embroidery floss or perle
cotton: orange or yellow

Ribbon

FINISHED MEASUREMENTS
5½ inches (14 cm) tall
Hat: 1¼ inches (3.2 cm) tall

1. Following steps 2–6 of Making Pompoms by Hand on pages 19–21, make a 2-inch (5.1 cm) round pompom from red yarn for the head. I used approximately ¼ skein of Patons medium-weight Classic Wool, which is approximately 53 yards (48 m).

2. Using the template on page 121, cut out a beak from orange wool felt.

3. Take the ball shape and locate where you want the beak to be. Make a small part into the pile of the yarn, squeeze in a small drop of glue, and insert the wool felt beak. Pinch the fibers around the glue and the beak to secure it. Let dry.

4. Using the inverted triangle layout (see Positioning the Nose and Eyes on page 22), decide where you want the eyes to be. Make a part in the yarn, carefully squeeze in a pea-size drop of glue for each eye, and gently insert the wire end of each glass eye into the pompom. Let the glue dry.

5. Make another slightly larger pompom from the brown yarn and trim it into an egg-shaped pompom for the body, about 3½ inches (8.9 cm) long. I used approximately ⅓ skein of Patons medium-weight Classic Wool, which is approximately 69 yards (63 m).

6. Glue the finished head onto the body. To create a cute, inquisitive expression, tilt the head to one side. Squeeze a nickel-size dollop of glue at the top of the body pompom and position the head as desired. You will need to let the glue set up and dry, which can take a while. To keep the head from falling off before the glue sets up, use a long floral pin to hold it in place. Remove the pin after the glue has set up and dried.

7. Using the template on page 122, cut out the tail pieces from the brown, beige, orange, and cream wool felts and glue them together with the smallest shape on top and the largest shape on the bottom.

8. At the tail end of the body make a part, squeeze in a bit of glue, and insert the tail. Pinch the wool fibers around the glue and the felt tail to secure them and let the glue dry.

9. Using wire cutters, cut eight 4-inch (10.2 cm) pieces of floral wire.

10. To create the legs, take four pieces of wire, hold them together, and lightly coat the bundle with glue. Working from top to bottom, wind the embroidery floss tightly and uniformly around the wires. Stop approximately 1½ inches (3.8 cm) from the bottom. Bend each of the four wires out at a 90° angle to make individual toes. Three will face forward; one will face backward to provide the support needed for the bird to stand. Continue wrapping each "toe" wire individually with embroidery floss to cover the floral wire. Repeat with the remaining four pieces of floral wire to create the other leg. Use wire cutters to snip off any excess wire length. Tuck any ends of embroidery thread underneath and let the glue dry.

11. At the bottom of the bird's body, make two separate parts into the wool plush for the legs and squeeze a dollop of glue into each. Insert the wire legs into the body. Pinch the wool fibers around the wrapped wires to secure them. Set the bird upright and make any necessary adjustments so that it can dry standing upright.

12. Create a little top hat for the Turkey: using the template on page 124, cut out the top hat shapes from dark brown felt. Apply a thin line of glue along one short end of the rectangle. Loop the rectangle to join both short ends together, creating a cylinder. Let the glue dry.

13. Apply a thin line of glue along one edge of the cylinder, and center the cylinder over the larger felt circle, gently pressing them together. Let the glue dry. Apply another thin line of glue along the remaining top edge of the cylinder. Place the smaller felt circle on top of the cylinder and allow the glue to dry.

14. Once the top hat's glue has dried, carefully trim an X in the bottom of the larger felt circle. Insert the tips of your scissors into the X and trim out the inside of the circle—this will allow the top hat to sit more fully upon the Turkey's head.

15. Tie a ribbon around the Turkey's neck.

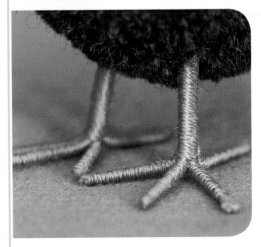

Snowman and Snowgirl

These cheerful snow people are sure to delight during the holiday season for generations to come. By changing a few little details, you can make either a snowgirl or a snowman, and if you're feeling ambitious, you could create an entire family of snow people.

1. Following steps 2–6 of Making Pompoms by Hand on pages 19–21, make three graduated sizes of pompoms using the white wool yarn. The top pompom should be about 2 inches (5.1 cm) in diameter; the middle pompom should be about 2½ inches (6.4 cm) in diameter; and the bottom pompom should be about 3 inches (7.6 cm). I used most of one skein of Patons medium-weight Classic Wool for the three pompoms: approximately ¼ skein, which is approximately 53 yards (48 m), for the head, and approximately ⅓ skein, or approximately 69 yards (63 m), for each of the two bottom pompoms.

2. Using a small marble-size bit of orange roving, needle felt a tiny carrot shape to use as the nose, about ½ inch (1.3 cm) long.

3. Locate where you want the nose to be on the smallest pompom and make a small part into the pile of the yarn. Place a small drop of glue in the part and insert the needle-felted carrot. Pinch the fibers around the carrot nose to secure it. Let dry.

4. Using the inverted triangle layout (see Positioning the Nose and Eyes on page 22), decide where you want the eyes to be. Make a part in the yarn, carefully squeeze in a pea-size drop of glue for each eye, and gently insert the wire end of each glass eye into the pompom. Let the glue dry.

5. To make the Snowgirl's felted arms, glue the pipe cleaner into the top half of the medium-size pompom. Simply make a horizontal part deep into the wool at the top, squeeze in a dime-size dollop of glue, and place the pipe cleaner snugly down into it; pinch the fibers of the wool yarn around the pipe cleaner to secure it. This will become the frame for the Snowgirl's arms, which you will needle felt. (See Creating Appendages on page 24.) Let the glue dry.

6. Trim and flatten the bottom of the smaller pompom head with your scissors. Trim and flatten the top and bottom of the middle-size pompom with your scissors. Repeat this step for the largest pompom as well. This creates the illusion that the snowballs have weight. Glue and stack all three pompoms together. Use floral pins to hold them together while they dry.

7. After the glue has fully dried, bend the Snowgirl's pipe cleaner into the desired position and trim each arm to approximately 3 inches (7.6 cm). Bend down and crimp the sharp ends of the pipe cleaners because they will poke through the needle-felted ends.

YOU WILL NEED

FOR BOTH THE SNOWMAN AND SNOWGIRL:
Basic Pompom Toolbox (page 12)

100% wool yarn: white

100% wool felt: white

100% wool roving: orange

2 black glass eyes, 10 or 12 mm (2 eyes for each)

3-inch (7.6 cm) flat wooden disk (1 disk for each)

Pale blue craft paint

Paintbrush

Clear glass glitter or mica

Scallop-edge scissors

FINISHED MEASUREMENTS
Snowman/Snowgirl:
5½ inches (14 cm) tall
(without pedestal or hat)

Snowman's hat:
1¼ inches (3.2 cm) tall

materials list continued on next page

Snowman and Snowgirl

100% wool felt: your choice of color(s) for a scarf and for the Snowman's top hat

Wire cutters, for trimming the Snowman's twig arms

Small twigs for the Snowman's arms, each approximately 2 1/2 inches (6.4 cm)

Template: top hat (page 124)

Velvet ribbon

3 black beads, 10 or 12 mm, for the Snowman's coal buttons

100% wool felt: your choice of color(s) for a scarf and for the Snowgirl's earmuff headband

100% wool roving: white for the Snowgirl's arms, your choice of color for the Snowgirl's earmuffs

6-inch (15.2 cm) white pipe cleaner, for the Snowgirl's arms

Needle felting supplies (page 16), for the Snowgirl's arms

Millinery flowers

Wrap a thick bacon-size strip of white roving tightly around the pipe cleaner armature from top to bottom. Needle felt the roving tightly to compact it around the pipe cleaner so it will not unravel (see Needle Felting Appendages on page 24).

8. Paint the 3-inch (7.6 cm) flat wooden disk with pale blue craft paint and let it dry. Coat the dry painted disk with glue and sprinkle clear glass glitter or mica over it; shake off the excess. Let the glue dry.

9. While the glue on the base dries, use the scallop-edge scissors to cut a circle of white felt measuring 3 1/2 inches (8.9 cm) in diameter. Adhere this felt circle to the bottom of the dry, painted disk.

10. Glue the snow person onto the center of the painted and glittered wooden disk. Let the glue dry.

11. For the Snowman's twig arms, use the wire cutters to cut two tiny twigs approximately 2 1/2 inches (6.4 cm) long. Make parts on each side in the middle pompom where you want the arms to be. Squeeze a bit of glue into each part and insert the twigs. Pinch the fibers around the twigs to secure them. Let dry.

12. Create a wool scarf by cutting a strip of wool felt approximately 1/2 x 7 inches (1.3 x 17.8 cm). Snip the ends to make the scarf's fringe. Wrap and tie it around your snow person's neck.

13. Embellish the Snowgirl with millinery flowers. To create her earmuffs, simply needle felt a 1-inch (2.5 cm) diameter ball of roving in any color of your choosing. Cut the ball in half. Cut a tiny strip of wool felt with the scallop-edge scissors for the earmuffs' headband. Glue the headband on the head and glue one ball half to each side of the head.

14. Using the template on page 124, cut out the Snowman's top hat shapes from felt. Apply a thin line of glue along one short end of the rectangle. Loop the rectangle to join both short ends together, creating a cylinder. Let the glue dry.

15. Apply a thin line of glue along one edge of the cylinder, and center the cylinder over the larger felt circle, gently pressing them together. Let the glue dry. Apply another thin line of glue along the remaining top edge of the cylinder. Place the smaller felt circle on top of the cylinder and allow the glue to dry.

16. Once the top hat's glue has dried, carefully trim an X in the bottom of the larger felt circle. Insert the tips of your scissors into the X and trim out the inside of the circle—this will allow the top hat to sit more fully upon the Snowman's head.

17. Cut a strip of velvet ribbon and glue it around the hat, just on top of the brim. Glue the small black beads (as the coal buttons) down the front of the Snowman.

✳ **NOTE:** *Add a nice wintry effect by lightly coating flowers and/ or berries with glue, dusting them with glass glitter or mica, and placing them as embellishments on the painted wooden disks or in the Snowman's or Snowgirl's hands.*

TEMPLATES

All templates are provided at 100%.

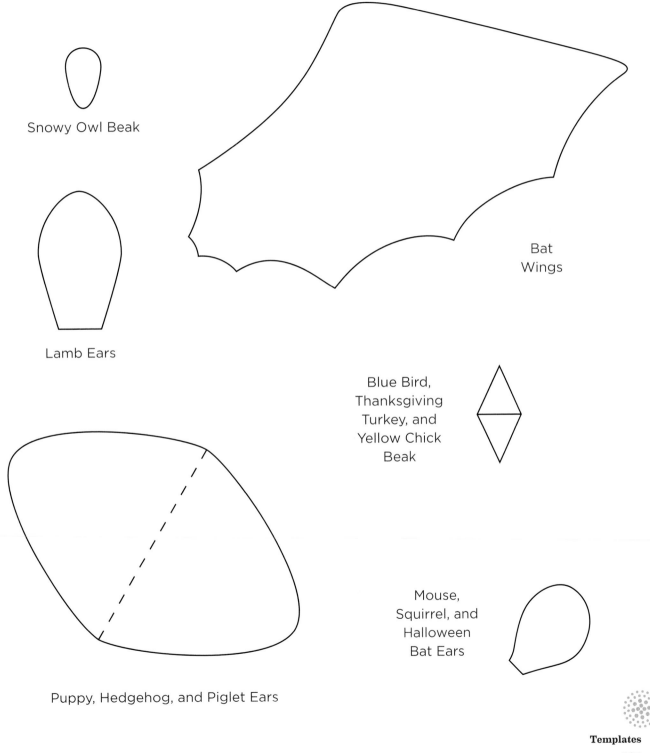

Snowy Owl Beak

Bat Wings

Lamb Ears

Blue Bird, Thanksgiving Turkey, and Yellow Chick Beak

Mouse, Squirrel, and Halloween Bat Ears

Puppy, Hedgehog, and Piglet Ears

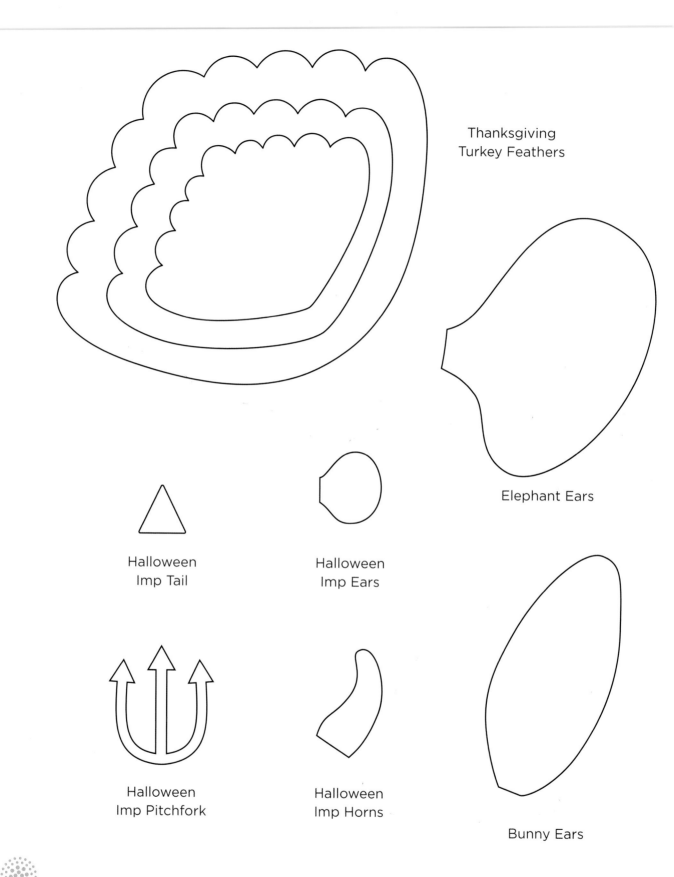

Thanksgiving
Turkey Feathers

Elephant Ears

Halloween
Imp Tail

Halloween
Imp Ears

Halloween
Imp Pitchfork

Halloween
Imp Horns

Bunny Ears

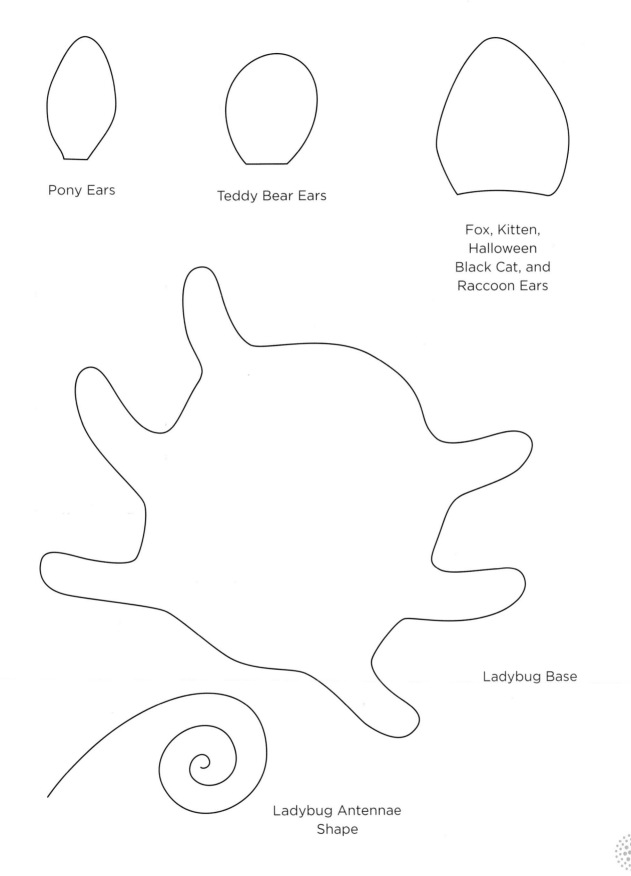

Pony Ears

Teddy Bear Ears

Fox, Kitten,
Halloween
Black Cat, and
Raccoon Ears

Ladybug Base

Ladybug Antennae
Shape

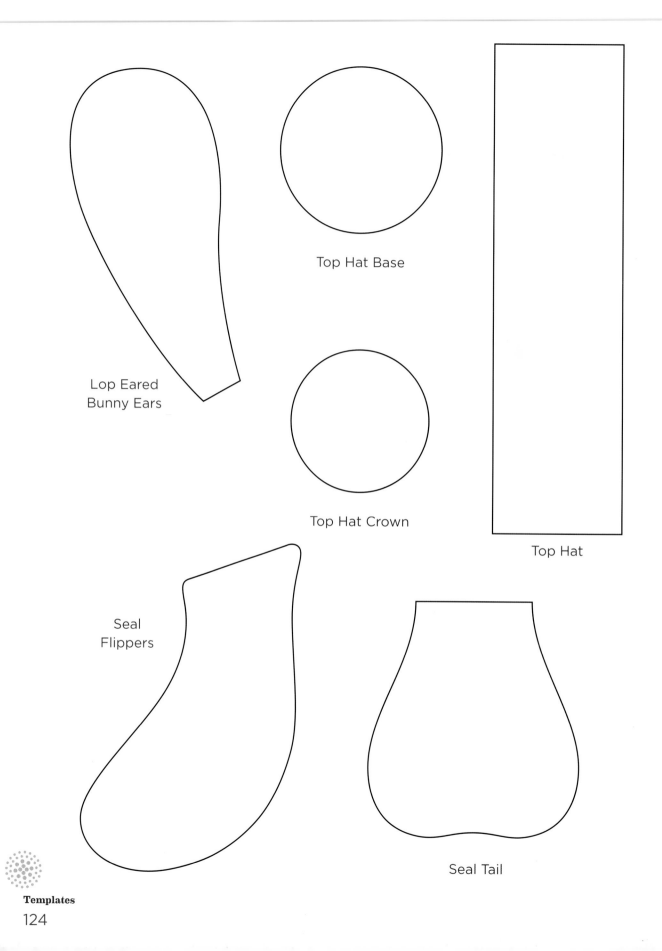

Lop Eared
Bunny Ears

Top Hat Base

Top Hat Crown

Top Hat

Seal
Flippers

Seal Tail

Resource List

Most of the tools and materials you'll need to make pompom creatures can be found in your local craft store, so here's a list of basic resource suggestions to get you started.

Yarn Supply and Needle Felting Supply

Patons
www.patonsyarns.com

Michaels
www.michaels.com

Jo-Ann Fabric and Craft Stores
www.joann.com

A.C. Moore Arts and Crafts
www.acmoore.com

Lion Brand Yarn
www.lionbrand.com

Red Heart Yarn
www.redheart.com

Additional Needle Felting Materials and Tools

Living Felt
www.livingfelt.com

The Felted Ewe
www.thefeltedewe.com

Clover
www.clover-usa.com

Paradise Fibers
www.paradisefibers.com

Millinery Supplies

Manny's Millinery Supply Company
www.shop.mannys-millinery.com

Judith M. Hats & Millinery Supplies
www.judithm.com

Glass Eyes

Glass Eyes Online
www.glasseyesonline.com

Hand Glass Craft
www.handglasscraft.com

G. Schoepfer Inc.
www.schoepferseyes.com

Shamrock Rose Teddy Bear Supplies
www.teddybearsupplies.flyingcart.com

About the Author

Myko Diann Bocek (pronounced Mike-o) is a designer, antique collector, mother, and student. Her half-Japanese heritage and her childhood experience growing up on a rural farm in Delaware both inform her love of vintage creations and all things cute.

Inspired by a television episode by fellow artist Jennifer Murphy on the *Martha Stewart Show* back in 2007, coupled with her love for vintage Steiff animals, Myko began making pompom animals during the evenings at home after work. She has since sold many of her original designs from her Etsy shop and she blogs at www.mykobocek.blogspot.com. She has been a featured craft artist in *Better Homes and Gardens' Holiday Crafts* magazine, as well as *Celebrate 365*. She currently lives in Arizona with her spouse and two youngest children (of four) and continues to create, collect, love, and learn. See more of Myko's work in her Etsy shop: www.etsy.com/shop/MykoBocekStudios.

Acknowledgments

I would like to thank my editor Beth Sweet for all of her help, guidance, and patience. Many thanks to Kristi Pfeffer for her wonderful design, to Michelle Owen for her artful layout, and to Jen Altman for capturing the expressive personality of each pompom creature in her photographs. Great applause goes to Kathy Brock for her copyediting wizardry. Thank you to Lark for giving me this opportunity. I am forever grateful.

Thank you to my childhood hero Beatrix Potter and artist Jennifer Murphy for giving me such inspiration and hope. Thank you to my husband, Brett, and to my dear friend Bill for your help and support. And last but not least, a huge thank you to my four amazing children, Shawn, Marina, Sierra, and Ian, who gave me the inspiration, willpower, and determination to create once again.

Index